传奇故事系列

麦格希 中英双语阅读文库

成长的烦恼
Growing Pains V
第5辑

[美]Deborah Ambroza ◎主编　　刘 慧　李晓东◎译

吉林出版集团有限责任公司

图书在版编目（CIP）数据

成长的烦恼. 第5辑 / (美) 安布罗西娅
(Ambroza,D.) 主编；刘慧，李晓东译. -- 长春：吉林
出版集团有限责任公司，2012.9
（麦格希中英双语阅读文库）
ISBN 978-7-5534-0420-2

Ⅰ.①成… Ⅱ.①安… ②刘… ③李… Ⅲ.①英语－
汉语－对照读物 Ⅳ.①H319.4

中国版本图书馆 CIP 数据核字(2012)第 205609 号

成长的烦恼 第5辑

主　　编：(美)Deborah Ambroza
翻　　译：刘　慧　李晓东
插　　画：齐　航　李延霞
责任编辑：于　鑫
封面设计：李立嗣
开　　本：650mm×960mm　1/16
字　　数：231千字
印　　张：10
版　　次：2013年1月第1版
印　　次：2015年4月第3次印刷

出　　版：吉林出版集团有限责任公司
发　　行：吉林出版集团外语教育有限公司
地　　址：长春市泰来街 1825 号
　　　　　邮编：130011
电　　话：总编办：0431-86012683
　　　　　发行部：0431-86012675　0431-86012826(Fax)
网　　址：www.360hours.com
印　　刷：北京一鑫印务有限责任公司

ISBN 978-7-5534-0420-2　定价：29.80 元

前言

英语思想家培根说过：阅读使人深刻。阅读的真正目的是获取信息，开拓视野和陶冶情操。从语言学习的角度来说，学习语言若没有大量阅读就如隔靴搔痒，因为阅读中的语言是最丰富、最灵活、最具表现力、最符合生活情景的，同时读物中的情节、故事引人入胜，进而能充分调动读者的阅读兴趣，培养读者的文学修养，至此，语言的学习水到渠成。

"麦格希中英双语阅读文库"在世界范围内选材，涉及科普、社会文化、文学名著、传奇故事、成长励志等多个系列，充分满足英语学习者课外阅读之所需，在阅读中学习英语、提高能力。

◎难度适中

本套图书充分照顾读者的英语学习阶段和水平，从读者的阅读兴趣出发，以难易适中的英语语言为立足点，选材精心、编排合理。

◎精品荟萃

本套图书注重经典阅读与实用阅读并举。既包含国内外脍炙人口、耳熟能详的美文，又包含科普、人文、故事、励志类等多学科的精彩文章。

◎功能实用

本套图书充分体现了双语阅读的功能和优势，充分考虑到读者课外阅读的方便，超出核心词表的词汇均出现在使其意义明显的语境之中，并标注释义。

鉴于编者水平有限，凡不周之处，谬误之处，皆欢迎批评教正。

我们真心地希望本套图书承载的文化知识和英语阅读的策略对提高读者的英语著作欣赏水平和英语运用能力有所裨益。

丛书编委会

Contents

1

Troika: Canine Superhero

I'm sure every boy loves his dog. If you ask any boy how much he loves his dog, he'll say, "More than anyone ever loved a dog before." But my dog is *different*. My dog is a superhero, and he became one even though he only had three legs. And I know for sure that I love my dog more than anyone has ever loved a dog before.

This dog was different from the day he was born. The other puppies in the *litter scrambled* over each other. They barked and whined and *growled*. But one dog was calm, as though he knew what

---

三腿狗：超级英雄狗

我敢保证每个男孩子都喜欢自己的狗，如果你问任何一个孩子是多么喜欢自己的狗，他一定会说，"要比任何人都爱自己的狗，"但我的狗是与众不同的，我的狗是一个超级英雄，虽然它只有三条腿，但它已经是一个英雄了。而且我非常确定地说，我比任何人都喜欢我的狗。

这条狗从一出生就与众不同，同一窝中的其他小狗都挤在一起，它们会吠叫、哀叫和嚎叫。但是有一只狗非常安静，它好像对周围的一切都

---

different *adj.* 不同的
scramble *v.* 爬

litter *n.* 一窝（幼崽）
growl *v.* 嚎叫

was going on. And when I held him, he looked me right in the eyes. It was as if he could speak. At the time, I couldn't think of a name that was good enough to fit him. So I just called him "Dog".

Dog only got better as he got older. He was the smartest of the litter, and by far the most loyal. The other dogs sleep outside in *doghouses*. But Dog couldn't fall asleep unless he was next to me. He would wait outside his doghouse all night. So he sleeps on the floor of my bedroom. We're never apart for a minute.

Dog and I live in Canada, above the *Arctic* Circle. Up here, there's snow on the ground for nine months of the year. There aren't many roads, and the rivers stay *frozen*. The sun doesn't even come up for a good part of the winter. My family and I use dogsleds to get around the frozen land.

非常明白。当我抱起它的时候，它看着我的眼睛，好像它能说话一样，这里我几乎想不出给它起什么名字最合适，所以我就叫它"狗狗"。

狗狗的年龄大一些后就会更好一些的，它是这窝狗中最聪明的一只，而且是目前最忠诚的一只。其他的狗都睡在狗窝的外面，但是狗狗不同，他必须在我的身边才能睡着。它会整个晚上等在狗窝的外面，所以它会睡在我卧室的门口，我们一分钟也不分离。

狗狗和我一起住在加拿大，在北极圈以内。这里的地面的积雪一年能保持九个月，这里没有道路，而且河流也是冻的。冬天很长的时间里太阳都不出来。我们全家和我利用狗雪撬在冰冻的地面上活动。

---

doghouse *n.* 狗窝
frozen *adj.* 冰冻的

Arctic *adj.* 北极的

It's hard to make a living u| here. If there's a *thaw* during the winter, it's *impossible* to cross the rivers by sled. Sometimes, food runs low, and we have to hunt deer, hares, and other animals.

During one thaw, I went out hunting. I had brought down a deer, and the dogs were resting while I cleaned it.

I realize now that it was my *fault*. I should have known that the thaw would bring some bears out of *hibernation*. I should have known that the smell of the deer would attract them. But I didn't think of it until the hungry bear had knocked me down, and by then, it was too late. I was staring straight down the throat of a huge grizzly.

But out of nowhere, Dog ripped free from his harness and leapt on the bear's back. The bear roared and twisted, but Dog held on. It

---

　　生活在这里很不容易，如果冬天出现冰雪融化的话，我们就无法用雪撬过河了。有时食物不够，我们必须猎鹿、兔等动物。

　　冰雪融化时，我要出去打猎，打到了一头鹿，我收拾鹿的时候，我的狗就在旁边等着。

　　我意识到这是我的错误，我应该知道，冰雪融化时，熊会从冬眠中醒来。我也应该知道鹿的味道会引来熊。但是只有熊把我弄倒后，我才想起来饥饿的熊，这时已经太晚了。我直盯盯地看这只灰熊的喉咙。

　　也不知道是从哪个方向，狗狗挣脱了挽具，跃向熊的后背，熊大叫着，挣扎着，但狗狗死咬不放。好像是长在了熊的身上，狗狗被熊的大爪

---

thaw *n.* 融化
fault *n.* 错误

impossible *adj.* 不可能的
hibernation *n.* 冬眠

all seemed to take forever. Dog was thrown by a *swipe* of the bear's huge paw, and the angry *creature* finally ran off.

I ran over to Dog. The wet snow was stained *scarlet* with his blood. His leg was bitten, badly, and I was sure the bone was broken. Dog could barely lift his head, but his eyes still told me that he was there for me.

I carried Dog home as quickly as I could. But his leg was badly hurt. My father had to amputate it. I was heartbroken—but Dog didn't seem to mind. Soon enough, he was back to being the best dog in the litter.

Even with three legs, Dog was still my strongest runner. The next winter, I started entering sled-dog races. Dog was always my lead dog. The other kids looked at me funny for having a three-legged lead dog. But they looked at me very differently when we won.

子掀了起来，然后这只愤怒的动物最后跑开了。

我跑到狗狗的面前，融化的冰雪上留下了它的斑斑血迹，它的腿被咬伤了，非常严重，我确定骨头被咬断了。狗狗抬不起头来，但它的眼神告诉我，他是来帮助我的。

我用最快的速度把狗狗带回家，但是它的腿受了重伤，爸爸必须给它截肢，我伤心极了，但是狗狗好像不是很在意。很快，它又变成了这窝狗中的最优秀的狗了。

狗狗虽然只有三条腿，但仍就是最能奔跑的，第二年冬天，我开始参加狗雪橇比赛，狗狗一直是我的领头狗。别的孩子奇怪地看着我用一只三条腿的狗当头狗，但是当我们赢得了比赛后，他们看我的眼光就不同了。

---

swipe *n.* 猛击   creature *n.* 动物
scarlet *n.* 鲜红色

After winning a few races, I entered my longest race yet. The course *stretched* over five hundred kilometers. I was one of the youngest people to enter, and the only person with a three-legged lead dog. But early on, Dog and I were in first place. The other racers even *commented* on how strong Dog seemed.

The hardest part of the race was a long stretch across a frozen river. The winds were bitter, and the ice could be *dangerous*. As the dogs ran, I could hear the river groaning and creaking under the ice.

Suddenly, the ice shuddered and cracked. Dog tugged hard, like he knew there was trouble. But the front of my sled caught on the crack, and it *tumbled* into the icy water.

The shock went through my whole body. I never thought anything could be so cold. I could barely see, and all I could do was hold on tight. Ahead of me, I saw dark shapes moving. And at the front of

---

赢过了几次比赛后，我进入了最长的比赛。比赛全程共有五百公里，我是比赛中最年轻的队员，而且是唯一有三条腿狗的队员。比赛开始时，我与狗狗保持在第一的位置，其他的队员还评论说狗狗是多么得强壮。

比赛最艰难的地方是穿过冰冻河的那一段，风刮得刺骨得冷，而且冰面非常危险，狗在上面跑时，我能听到下面的河发出的哀鸣声和裂开的声音。

突然，冰在颤抖，裂开了。狗狗用力地向前拖，如像它知道出了问题一样，但雪撬的前端卡在冰裂开处，翻进了冰冷的水里。

我的整个身体都在发抖，我从来没想过有这么冷的东西，我几乎什么东西都看不清，我只能紧紧地抓住雪撬，在我的眼前，只能感到有狗狗

---

stretch *v.* 延伸；绵延

dangerous *adj.* 危险的

comment *v.* 评论

tumble *v.* 摔倒；跌落

those dark shapes was Dog. He kept tugging, no matter what. At last, the team was able to drag the sled out of the water. He had saved me again.

I spent the whole night by the fire, and I thought I might never be warm or dry again. But Dog *curled* up next to me. He kept me warm all night. By the next morning, we were ready to go again.

I thought that was the last of our *troubles*. The next morning dawned bright and cold, and we were running hard. It wasn't long before we were at the head of the pack again. And Dog, as always, was right up front.

During a short rest, Dog's ears suddenly pricked up. There was a crashing sound coming from the trees. A huge bull *moose* stumbled into the clearing where we were. Nothing scares me more than

---

的一个影子。它不停地拖着，什么都不在乎。最后这群狗把雪撬拉出了水面，狗狗又一次地救了我的命。

我在火边待了一个晚上，我以为我不可能再变得温暖和干燥了，但是狗狗趴在我的身边儿，一晚上它让我保持着温暖，第二天早上，我们又能出发了。

我觉得这是我们最后一个麻烦了，第二天早晨天空明亮而寒冷，我们拼命地向前跑，没用多久我们又跑到了比赛队伍的前面。狗狗和以前一样，跑在最前面。

我们做一个短短的休息，这时狗狗的耳朵竖了起来，树林里传来了哗啦啦的声音，一头巨大的公麋鹿趔趔趄趄地奔向我们的空地。我最怕麋

---

curl *v.* 卷曲

moose *n.* 麋鹿

trouble *n.* 麻烦

moose. Unlike bears, they're *unpredictable*. They seem to get mad and charge for no reason.

The moose sent a puff of steam out of its *nostrils*. Then, with a grunt, it started to gallop toward us. This was a *disaster*. The moose was about to *trample* me and my entire sled-dog team. But like a shot, Dog leapt at the moose and seized its leg.

The moose gave a mighty kick. It was too much even for Dog, who went sailing through the air. He hit a tree, hard, and I was sure he was dead. The moose lowered its head and seemed to eye the rest of the dogs. But Dog got up. He stood swaying on his three legs. And he stared that moose in the eyes until the moose realized that Dog would never, never give up. Looking a little frightened, the moose retreated into the woods.

鹿，它们的行为很难预测，还容易发怒，而且毫无原因地发起攻击。

麋鹿从鼻孔中喘出热气，然后大叫了一声，向我们冲来，这是一场灾难。就当麋鹿要踩到我和整个雪撬狗队伍的时候，狗狗像箭一样，跃向麋鹿，咬住了麋鹿的腿。

麋鹿使出全身的力气一踢，这让狗狗难以忍受，被甩到了半空，重重地撞在一棵树上，我认为它被撞死了，麋鹿低下了头，看着其他的狗。但是狗狗又站了起来，它用三条腿站了起来，有些摇晃，双眼直盯着麋鹿的眼睛，直到麋鹿意识到这只狗永远不会让步的。麋鹿有些胆怯了，于是退到了树林里去了。

---

unpredictable *adj.* 无法预测的   nostril *n.* 鼻孔
disaster *n.* 灾难   trample *v.* 踩踏

That was the third time my three-legged dog had saved my life. After that, I knew what I would name him.

I chose the word Troika. It's a Russian word that *refers to* things that come in threes. And even though he only has three legs, he has *proven* three times that he is a true superhero.

这是我的这只三条腿的狗第三次救了我的命。从此以后，我知道我必须给它起个名子。

我挑了三腿狗这个词儿，这是一个俄语词儿，意思是以"三"为一组出现的事物，而且虽然它只有三条腿，但是它三次证明它是一个超级的英雄。

---

refer to 提到   prove *v.* 证明

2

The Nor'easter

"**S**ome weather for *Thanksgiving*, eh Kevin?" Grandma said, her voice seeming to *literally* break the ice in the freezing living room. It was silent except for three sounds: the creaking of the house straining against the wind, the whick, whick of Grandma's knife as she *whittled* another of her wooden *dwarfs*, and Kevin's teeth chattering.

"Not a good night for people to be out," she murmured, almost to herself.

东北风暴

"**过**感恩节遇上了这么一个天气，哎，凯文？"奶奶说，她的声音简直能把这个寒冷的房间里的冰给打破。除了有三个声音外，一切都是寂静：风挤进屋子发出的吱吱声，奶奶用刀削她的另一个木头小人的咔咔声，还有凯文牙齿发出的嗒嗒声。

"对于屋外的人来说，这个晚上可真不好，"她嘟囔着，几乎是自言自语。

Thanksgiving *n.* 感恩节
whittle *v.* 削

literally *adv.* 简直
dwarf *n.* 矮子

Kevin and his parents had left their apartment in Boston extra early that morning, because it was beginning to *sleet*. By the time they got on the *highway*, it was nearly a *blizzard*, cars *fishtailing* everywhere until the whole highway slowed to thirty-five miles an hour. The two-hour trip to Cape Cod ended up taking six, and they assumed they would be the last to arrive. But as soon as they stepped into Grandma's wonderful smelling but chilly entryway, she called from the kitchen:

"Uncle Bob and his new wife are stuck in a ditch out on the turnpike, and the tow truck's so busy it can't get to them for an hour. They asked if you'd pick them up in your four wheel drive."

"You stay here, Kevin," his father had instructed, and Kevin groaned. Without his cousins around, the only thing to do at

---

凯文和爸爸妈妈今天早晨非常早就离开了波士顿的公寓，因为天很快就要下雨夹雪了。当他们到了高速公路时，几乎是暴风雪了，汽车左右摇摆，结果是整个高速公路的速度下降到每小时35英里。到达科德角这两个小时的旅程，实际上用了6个小时，他们以为自己是最后一个到达的，但是当他们走进奶奶家的味道鲜美，但略有凉爽的通道时，从厨房里传出奶奶的声音：

"鲍勃叔叔和他的新娘在公路收费口那里掉进了一个泥坑中，拖车现在特别忙，需要一个小时才可能到他们那里，他们问你们能不能开你们的四轮驱动车去接他们。"

"你在这里待着，凯文，"他的爸爸已经提出要求，凯文哼了一声，

---

sleet *v.* 下雨夹雪　　　　　　　　highway *n.* 高速公路
blizzard *n.* 暴风雪　　　　　　　　fishtail *v.* （车辆）摆尾行驶

Grandma's house was listen to another one of her stories.

"Not a good night at all," she muttered, the knife *scratching* as she etched the dwarf's beard. "When I was a girl we had a Nor'easter like this right around the holidays, must've been twice as bad as this one. You hear that wind groaning, Kevin? Well, that isn't the worst of it."

As if *disagreeing* with her, the wind suddenly gusted against the house, pounding like an *enormous* fist on all the windows. Outside, Kevin could see the snow sweeping through the single cone-shaped beam of light from the streetlamp.

"There's something called the storm swell that happens when the air pressure drops at the center of the storm," Grandma continued. "It *sucks up* a huge dome of water, like God was holding a giant

---

如果没有表弟在，在奶奶家唯一能做的就是再听奶奶的一个故事。

"这个夜晚一点儿都不好，"她嘟囔着，传来刻小人胡子时的沙沙声。"我还是个小姑娘时，我在假期快到的时候赶上过一个很像这样的东北风暴，比这个要坏上两倍，你是不是听到风的呼啸了，凯文?好的，这还不算坏呢。"

风像故意与奶奶做对，突然猛吹房子，像一个巨大的拳头敲击着窗户。凯文看到外面的大雪，透过街灯上的锥形光线漫卷。

"当暴风雪中心的气压下降时，就会发生一种叫做风暴涌浪的东西，"奶奶接着说，"它会吸起像巨大圆顶一样的水，如同上帝在海洋上用一个

---

scratch *v.* 发出刮擦声
enormous *adj.* 巨大的

disagree *v.* 不同意
suck up 吸

vacuum cleaner over the ocean. Comes in at high tide and you've got flooding like you can't *imagine*."

"This storm swell came in at evening tide," she continued. "My father herded us all upstairs where we watched the ocean from the big bay windows in Mother and Father's bedroom. First the spray came across the road and began to wet the paint on our neighbor's, the MacIntosh's, house. Then the water came up to the top of their *foundation*, and the waves were creeping up our front walk. Then we heard them slap, slapping against the house; sometimes a big one came along, and whoosh! We'd hear it *drumming* against the walls."

The wind seemed to be listening, for it echoed the noise of the waves. Kevin gasped and looked quickly out the window, imagining

---

巨大的吸尘器，乘着涨潮的潮水过来，这里的洪水是无法想象的。"

"每个潮汐都会有风暴涌浪，"她接着说，"我爸爸把我们一起带到楼上，我们从父母卧室的一个大的飘窗上看着大海。开始是水花从街道的对面飞过来，把我们的邻居马金托什家房子外面的油漆弄湿，然后是水漫过房基，再就是浪爬上房前的小路。我们会听到啪啪声，不停地拍着我们的房子。有时会有一个大浪，嗖一声！我听到浪已经撞到我们的墙上了。"

风可能是在听我们说话，因为它在回应着浪的声音。凯文倒吸ㄕ一口

---

vacuum *n.* 吸尘器   imagine *v.* 想象
foundation *n.* 房基   drum *v.* 有规律地敲击

for a moment that the blowing snow was the white *fringe* of a wave crashing against the house.

"The waves kept rising, and one by one we heard our windows *smash* out. Front door busted open and the water poured into the living room; we could hear our *furniture* bumping into things as it bobbed around, hear the water slopping up the stairs."

"Father was about to take us up to the attic when we heard this *awful* crashing noise. We looked out the window, and the MacIntosh's house had been ripped right off its foundation, creaking and groaning as it floated away. Then like a sinking ship, it spun and tipped over, crash! I was friends with the little MacIntosh girl, Amy. She and her mom grabbed onto the couch and ended up on the

---

凉气，快速向窗处看去，此时他想象着被风吹起来的雪就像白色边缘浪撞击在房子上一样。

"浪不断地升高，我们听到我们的窗户一个个被打碎，前门被吹得大开，水流进起居室，我们能听到家具在水中到处漂着，碰在别的东西上，听到了水顺着楼梯而上。"

"父亲刚要把我们带到阁楼，我们就听到可怕的的嘶嘶声，我们向窗外看去，马金托什的房子从房基开始被抬了起来，一边漂走一边发出尖叫和低鸣的声音。然后，就像一个要沉的船一样，旋转着、翻了，咔嚓一声！我与马金托什家的女孩，埃米是好朋友。她和她妈妈抓住了一个沙

---

fringe *n.* 边缘
furniture *n.* 家具

smash *v.* 打碎
awful *adj.* 可怕的

beach in Tonset, alive. They never saw her father or brother again."

Suddenly there was a *horrible* screaming sound, and Kevin leapt about two feet into the air.

"Pie's done!" Grandma announced, getting to her feet and shuffling into the kitchen—it was only the oven timer. Her voice floated out of the kitchen with the warm smell of cinnamon. "Not scaring you, am I? Heck, I'm scared myself; no good having all your children out in weather like this."

Kevin walked to the window and *cupped* his hands over his eyes. The only thing *visible* was the cone of falling snow under the *streetlamp*. He imagined that outside that bit of light, the waves were

---

发，最后漂到了通塞特的海边，都还活着。她们再也没有见到她的爸爸和哥哥。"

突然传来一阵可怕的哭叫声，凯文在空中跳了有两英尺远。

"饼已经做好了！"奶奶认真地说，站起身来，拖着脚走进厨房——这只是烤炉的定时器。她的声音从厨房里飘了出来，带有肉桂的暖味。"我吓到你了吧?是不是?真见鬼，我把自己都吓着了，这样的天气，让你们这些孩子在外面不怎么好。"

凯文来到了窗前，把手环起来放在眼睛前，唯一能看清的东西就是街灯下面锥形的飘雪。他想像着光线以外的的部分，浪开始爬上了海岸，正

---

horrible *adj.* 可怕的
visible *adj.* 可见的

cup *v.* 使成环状
streetlamp *n.* 路灯

beginning to crawl up the shore, lapping toward the house.

Yes, there it was—he was sure he saw the white edge of a wave slipping onto the road, *splashing* into bright flecks of spray. His heart pounded as the shape shifted and grew, and just before he was about to run to his grandmother, he realized what he saw: *headlights*. The lights from a car shone on the enormous *snowflakes*, making them look like the moving front of a wave. It was his parents' car pulling into the *driveway*, with Bob and Nancy in the back seat. Kevin laughed at himself, and ran to the door to welcome them in from the storm.

在舔舐着房子。

是的，真地舔舐着，他确信他看到了白边儿的浪溜上了路面，溅起闪闪的水花。这些东西变化着形状，不断地变大，他的心咚咚地跳着。在他要跑向奶奶时，他意识到看到的东西是车的前灯。车灯照在巨大的雪片上，看起来就像滚动的浪的前峰。他父母的车慢慢地开进了车道，鲍勃和南希坐在车的后坐上。凯文对自己笑了一下，跑到前门去接从暴风雪中回来的人们。

---

splash *v.* （使）飞溅
snowflake *n.* 雪花

headlight *n.* 车前灯
driveway *n.* 车道

3

Mystery at Camp White Cloud

Frankie, Gil, and Angela

Frankie looked over the book she was reading to see a group of children choosing teams on the soccer field. Behind them stood a brown wooden arch with the *faded* words "Welcome to *Camp White Cloud*."

Frankie (short for Francis, which she *disliked*) had arrived yesterday, along with 199 other campers, to spend two weeks in the mountains of Colorado.

白云营地的秘密

弗兰吉、吉尔和安杰拉

弗兰吉从书上抬起眼睛，看着足球场上的孩子们正在选自己的队员。在运动场的后面是一个黄色的木拱门，上面的字有些退色："欢迎来到白云宿营地"。

弗兰吉（是弗朗西斯的简称，她不喜欢这个名字）是昨天与199个其他宿营的孩子一块儿来的，将在科罗拉多的山区过上两周的生活。

---

fade *v.* 退色　　　　　　　　　　　　　　　　　camp *n.* 营地
dislike *v.* 不喜欢

"Hey Frankie! How's it going?" came a voice from behind her.

"Oh, hi Gil. I'm fine. How are you?" Gil was the first camper Frankie had met yesterday.

A loud cheer *interrupted* them. A tall girl wearing a Camp White Cloud T-shirt was jumping up and down, celebrating the goal she scored.

"Have you met Angela Hansen yet?" Gil asked.

"She's in my *cabin*. Everybody knows her," Frankie answered.

Gil thought for a moment. "You know, it must be great to be Angela. Her dad is Camp *Director*. She gets to play all summer."

"Yeah, but he's always busy running the camp, she probably doesn't see her dad much," Frankie said.

"喂，弗兰吉！怎么样?"从她身后传来了一个声音问。

"噢，喂，吉尔，我很好，你怎么样?"吉尔是弗兰吉昨天第一个遇到的宿营孩子。

一阵大声的欢笑声打断了她们，一个穿着白云宿营地T恤衫的高个子女孩蹦跳着，庆祝自己进了一个球。

"你见到了安杰拉·汉森吗?"吉尔问。

"她与我住在一个小屋里，谁都认识她，"弗兰吉回答说。

吉尔想了一会儿，"你知道，作为安杰拉一定很了不起，她爸爸是营地的主任，她能在这里玩一个暑假。"

"是的，但是他为了管理这个营地，总是很忙，也许她很少能看到她的爸爸，"弗兰吉说。

---

interrupt *v.* 打断   cabin *n.* 小屋
director *n.* 主任

A bell suddenly chimed, and the soccer game stopped.

"Lunch, let's go eat—I'm *starving*!" Gil said as he jumped up from the rock.

Bump Goes the Night

That night, Frankie lay on her bunk after lights out. She thought of the story of Old Man Looper that Angela told earlier.

Looper was a miner who hoped to find a fortune in gold in the area's mountain streams. *Unfortunately*, he had little luck and started talking only to himself and his mule. One day, he *mysteriously* disappeared; Angela said he'd *haunted* the camp ever since.

这时突然响起铃声，足球比赛也停了下来。

"午餐了，我们吃饭去吧——我都要饿死了！"吉尔从岩石上蹦下来说。

不平静的一夜

那天晚上熄灯以后，弗兰吉躺在自己的床铺上，她想起来安杰拉跟她讲过的卢珀老头儿的故事。

卢珀是一个采矿工，他希望能在山里的小溪中找到黄金而发财。但是他没有那么幸运，他开始只和自己还有他的驴说话。有一天，他神秘地消失了，安杰拉说从此以后他就在营地里出没。

---

starve *v.* 饥饿
mysteriously *adv.* 神秘地

unfortunately *adv.* 不幸地
haunt *v.* 常出没于

Frankie didn't believe the story. It was just meant to *scare* new campers, she thought, as she drifted off to sleep.

"WHAT WAS THAT?!" a voice called out. Frankie shot up in her bunk.

"Shhh! Listen!" someone whispered from a lower bunk.

Hearing a twig snap, Frankie caught *a glimpse of* a *shadow* outside the cabin.

"Hey, Michiko! I think it's coming toward your window!" Frankie whispered *urgently*.

"I don't see anything," Michiko answered.

弗兰吉不相信这个故事，她认为这只是为了吓唬这些宿营的孩子们，她渐渐地进入了梦乡。

"这到底是什么……?"一个声音大叫到。弗兰吉在她的床铺上喊了起来。

"嘘!小心听着!"下铺有人压低了嗓音说。

弗兰吉听到了一个树枝折断的声音，她看到小屋外面的一个影子。

"喂，米希科!我想它朝你的窗户去了!"弗兰吉焦急地小声说。

"我什么都没有看到，"米希科回答说。

---

scare *v.* 吓唬
shadow *n.* 影子

a glimpse of 看一眼
urgently *adv.* 焦急地

Everyone in the cabin held their breath. Frankie could *faintly* see Angela's bunk; she couldn't believe Angela was sleeping through this.

"Where is it now?" Frankie asked.

"I think it's moving away from us," Michiko said.

"Toward the boys' cabin?" Frankie asked.

"I think so," Michiko said.

After a few more questions, everyone quieted down. The image *lurking* outside the cabin frightened Frankie, but it also raised questions. The big one being: Why would someone, or something, be outside their cabin at this hour?

　　小屋内的每一个人都屏住呼吸，弗兰吉能够模糊地看到安杰拉的床铺，她真的不感相信安杰拉能在这样的条件下睡觉。

　　"它到哪里去了？"弗兰吉问。

　　"我想可能是离开我们了，"米希科说。

　　"向男孩子的小屋去了？"弗兰吉问。

　　"我想可能是，"米希科说。

　　大家又提出了几个问题后，都安静了下来。窗外潜伏的影子让弗兰吉很是害怕，但也引出了一串问题，其中最大的问题是：为什么在这个时间里在他们的小屋外面，出现了一个人或一个东西？

---

faintly *adv.* 模糊地　　　　　　　　　　　　　　　　lurk *v.* 潜伏

First Warning

"Hey Gil, did you boys see anything last night?" Frankie asked after *breakfast*.

"Yes! It was crazy. We all saw something sneaking around our cabin, *scratching* and moving around," Gil answered.

"So, what do you think it was?" Frankie continued.

"I really don't know," he said, "What do you think, Angela?"

"I was asleep; but it had to be Old Man Looper," Angela said. "He *shows up* every summer."

Still, Frankie *refused to* believe it was Looper.

A bell signaled morning activity time. Angela and Gil went to

---

第一次警告

"喂，吉尔，你们男孩子昨晚看到什么没有？"弗兰吉吃完早饭问。

"看到了，真奇怪了，我们都看到有东西藏在我们小屋的附近，乱拿乱抓而且到处跑，"吉尔回答说。

"那么，你想它是什么呢？"弗兰吉接着问。

"我真的不知道，"她说，"你认为呢，安杰拉？"

"我睡着了，但是它一定是卢珀这个老头儿，"安杰拉说，"每年夏天他都出现。"

然而，弗兰吉不接受这是卢珀。

铃声响了，这是告诉大家这是早晨的活动时间。安杰拉和吉尔去了木

---

breakfast *n.* 早餐　　　　　　　　　　　　　　　scratch *v.* 抓
show up 出现　　　　　　　　　　　　　　　　　refuse to 拒绝

woodworking class, and Frankie went to kayaking class.

Walking back to the cabin after kayaking, Frankie heard loud voices ahead of her.

"Come over here, you guys! Look at this!"

Carved *roughly* into the wooden planks were the words: "THIS IS NOT YOUR HOME! LEAVE NOW!"

"OK, now I'm really starting to worry," Michiko *admitted*.

"Me too," Frankie said quietly.

Last Chance

The next morning during cabin clean-up time, Frankie heard *excited* voices coming from the dining hall.

工教室，弗兰吉去了皮艇运动教室。

从皮艇运动教室到小屋，弗兰吉在她前方听到了一个声音。

"都到这里来，你们这些人！看看这个！"

在木板上粗糙地刻着这些字："这不是你的家！现在就离开！"

"好吧，现在我真的有些担心了，"米希科承认说。

"我也是，"弗兰吉平静地说。

最后一次机会

第二天早晨的房间清理时间，弗兰吉听到从餐厅里传来激动的声音。

---

roughly *adv.* 粗糙地　　　　　　　　　　　　　　admit *v.* 承认
excited *adj.* 激动的

When Frankie arrived at the building, she let out a gasp. Inside the dining hall was a *mess* and one wall was carved with "LAST WARNING! LEAVE NOW!".

Frankie was *surrounded* by excited voices and questions.

"Who did this?"

"Do you think it's Looper?"

"Why would he want us gone?"

The voices quickly faded as Director Hansen entered the dining hall.

"OK, OK campers, back to your cabins. I know you're all concerned, but I'll figure out what's going on."

弗兰吉到了大楼时，她长出了一口气，餐厅里面一片混乱，墙上刻着"最后一次警告！现在就离开！"。

弗兰吉的周围都是兴奋的声音和问题。

"谁做的这件事呢？"

"你想那是卢珀吗？"

"他为什么让我们离开呢？"

汉森主任走进了餐厅，声音很快就消失了。

"好的，好的，宿营的孩子们，回到你们的小屋里去，我知道你们都很关心，但是我会搞清楚是怎么回事儿的。"

---

mess *n.* 混乱　　　　　　　　　　　　　　　surround *v.* 包围

Camp *Calamity*

Later, as Frankie's cabin-mates ate dinner, Michiko asked, "Has anyone seen Frankie or Gil?"

No one had seen them since they were ordered back to their cabins. Suddenly, the *loudspeakers crackled* to life. The campers yelped in surprise; it was already creepy being in the dining hall after what had happened to it.

"Attention campers, there will be a *mandatory* all-camp meeting in 10 minutes."

Word spread quickly that Frankie and Gil were missing.

营地灾难

后来，弗兰吉同屋的女孩子们吃早饭时，米希科问，"有人看到弗兰吉或者吉尔了吗？"

从她们被命令回到小屋以后，没有人见过她们。突然，高音喇叭大声地响了起来。宿营的孩子们惊讶地大叫了起来。经过了所发生的这些事情后，待在餐厅就让人感觉到后背发凉。

"宿营的孩子们请注意，十分钟后我们有一个全营地会议，人人必须到会。"

很快有传言说，弗兰吉和吉尔不见了。

---

calamity *n.* 灾难　　　　　　　　　　loudspeaker *n.* 高音喇叭
crackle *v.* 噼啪作响　　　　　　　　mandatory *adj.* 命令的

Ten minutes later, Director Hansen spoke *gravely*. "For the first time in its 40-year history, Camp White Cloud will be closing early."

"WAIT, DIRECTOR HANSEN!"

All heads turned to see Frankie and Gil *sprinting* toward them.

"Frankie! Gil! Where have you been?" asked Director Hansen.

Frankie walked up to Director Hansen and whispered into his ear. After a few moments, Director Hansen *straightened* up.

"White Cloud Campers," he began. "I have some great news! Thanks to Frankie and Gil, Camp White Cloud stays open!"

十分钟以后，汉森主任严肃地说，"这是白云宿营地开业40年来的第一次，我们要提前关闭。"

"请等一下，汉森主任！"

所有的脑袋都转了过来，弗兰吉和吉尔飞一样地朝他们跑过来。

"弗兰吉！吉尔！你们到哪里去了？"汉森主任问。

弗兰吉走近了汉森主任，向他的耳朵里小声地说了些什么，几分钟以后，汉森主任直起腰来。

"白云宿营地的孩子们，"他开始说，"我有一个最好的消息！多亏弗兰吉和吉尔，白云宿营地，还要继续开放！"

---

gravely *adv.* 严肃地   sprint *v.* （短距离）冲刺
straighten *v.* 变直

Epilogue

In his office, Director Hansen asked Frankie how she and Gil figured out Angela frightened everyone.

"I remembered Angela didn't wake up when the *prowler* came," Frankie said. "She must have stuffed her sleeping bag with pillows."

"And Angela left woodworking early; she said she was feeling sick," Gil said.

"The dining hall—she must have done that by *sneaking out* while everyone was sleeping," Frankie said.

"Then we went looking for clues and found a letter addressed to you, sir, in her woodworking box," Frankie said. "That's when we really realized how upset she was."

后记

在汉森的办公室，他问弗兰吉是怎样与吉尔一起看出来是安杰拉吓唬别人的。

"我想起来了，在潜行者进来的时候，安杰拉没有醒过来，"弗兰吉说，"她一定是把她的睡袋用枕头塞起来了。"

"而且安杰拉很早就离开了木工教室了，她说自己不舒服。"吉尔说。

"餐厅——这是她趁大家睡觉时偷偷做的，"弗兰吉说。

"然后我们去找线索，在她的木工工艺箱中发现一个写给你的信，先生，"弗兰吉说。"到那时，我们知道她是多么烦恼。"

---

epilogue *n.* 后记

sneak out 溜出去

prowler *n.* 潜行者

Angela looked up at her father. "Daddy, I'm so sorry. I know it was wrong."

"Oh, Angela, I'm sorry, too," Director Hansen said.

Angela *continued* with tears in her eyes, "I know how important you are to all of these campers, but I just couldn't *stand* not getting time with you any more."

"It's OK—it's a good thing we had *detectives* like Frankie and Gil to solve the case."

安杰拉抬头看了一下她的爸爸，"爸爸，我真的对不起，我知道错了。"

"噢，安杰拉，我也对不起，"汉森主任说。

安杰拉眼含泪水接着说，"我知道你对这些宿营的孩子们多么重要，但我不能再忍受没有时间和你在一起。"

"不要紧的，这是一件很好的事情，我们有像弗兰吉和吉尔一样的探长来解决这个案子。"

---

continue *v.* 继续

detective *n.* 探长

stand *v.* 忍受

4

Yosemite and the Badge

Bookstore *Treasure*

I watched Nana wind through the busy city streets with her favorite scarf *wrapped* tight. Her face was stern as she moved through the crowds of people with a book in her hand. Then she saw me, looking through the window down at her, and smiled. It turned out the book was for me. It was a Junior Ranger Handbook for Yosemite National Park, and before dinner I was *halfway* through it!

约塞米蒂国家公园与臂章

从书店带回的财富

我看见祖母戴着她最喜欢的围巾，穿过城市繁忙的街道。她拿着书从人群中穿过，满面严肃。不一会儿，她发现我在楼上透过窗户看她，她朝我笑了一下。后来才知道那本书是给我的。书是写给约塞米蒂国家公园的少年看守员的手册。晚餐前，我就已经看完了一半。

---

treasure *n.* 财富   wrap *v.* 包

halfway *adv.* （事情）进行到中途

Although Nana hated bugs and trees and bushes and bears, she knew I loved the outdoors, and it meant a lot that she would find a book just for me.

After I finished the book, I put it on my shelf next to some other books by my favorite author, John Muir, the famous *conservationist* and *naturalist*. He did so much to *conserve* nature that some people call him the father of our national park system.

That night I could barely sleep. The activities in the *Junior Ranger* book kept running through my mind. It said that the more activities I did, the closer I would be to earning the official Junior Ranger badge. I wanted that badge. I thought how proud John Muir might have been to know that a kid could help *preserve* Yosemite years after he had written about the need for people to preserve it.

尽管祖母很讨厌小虫子、森林、灌木丛以及熊，但是她知道我喜欢户外，所以她为我特别找出一本书实在是意义重大。

我看完整本书之后，将其放在我的书架上，一旁是我最喜欢的作者，约翰·缪尔的书。约翰·缪尔是著名的环保主义者和自然主义者。他为了保护自然付出了很多，有人称他为我们国家公园的系统之父。

那晚，我翻来覆去睡不着。《少年守护者》那本书里的任务不时涌入我的脑海。书中说，做的任务越多，便离得到那枚"少年守护者"臂章越近。我很想要那枚臂章。我想，约翰·缪尔要是知道有个小孩读到了他数年前呼吁人们保护约塞米蒂的书便去保护那里，一定会非常自豪的。

---

conservationist *n.* 环保主义者
conserve *v.* 保护

naturalist *n.* 自然主义者
preserve *v.* 保护

John Muir, a naturalist, *geologist*, and more, argued in the late 1800s that the natural beauty of Yosemite must be saved for future generations to see.

The next morning, I woke up early, pulled the new book off the shelf, and started to do the activities.

First, I did the word find; then, I drew a "Save the Bears" *poster*, which I presented to Nana. She smiled and said, "That's nice."

Then I asked her, "Nana, I really want the Junior Ranger badge, but to get it I have to go to Yosemite National Park and *complete* some more activities. Will you take me?"

Nana shook her head. "You know how I hate the outdoors."

Then I think she saw the look of *disappointment* on my face

约翰·缪尔，自然主义者，地质学者，等等，在十九世纪末期主张保护约塞米蒂的自然风光，以便后代能欣赏到此等美景。

第二天，我醒得很早，把那本书从书架上拿下来，开始行动。

首先，我查了一下字数，然后做了张"拯救黑熊"的海报。我把这张海报给祖母看，她笑了笑，说，"画得不错。"

我问她："祖母，我真的很想要'少年守护者'臂章，但是我只有去约塞米蒂国家公园然后完成更多的任务才能得到，你愿意带我去吗？"

祖母摇摇头，"你知道我有多讨厌户外。"

之后，我想她是看到了我脸上的失望之情，因为她说："好吧，你生

---

geologist *n.* 地质学者
complete *v.* 完成

poster *n.* 海报
disappointment *n.* 失望

because she said, "Well, you do have a birthday coming up. I was going to get you that *stereo* you wanted but, I guess if we watched our *pennies* and camped out, a trip to Yosemite wouldn't cost much more."

That weekend, Nana and I packed the car with a cooler of drinks and food, sleeping bags, *pillows*, and blankets. Although Nana was a real trooper about it all, I knew she would rather stay in a hotel than go camping.

Lightning strikes in and around Yosemite in June this year caused nine fires in the park.

Over the River

About an hour before we arrived at the park, we had to take a

---

日马上就到了，我本来想给你买那个你想要的立体音响的，但是我想，如果我们节省点，在外露营的话，去约塞米蒂也不会花多少钱。"

那个周末，我和祖母在车上装满了冷饮和食物、睡袋、枕头，还有毯子。尽管祖母是一个真正的骑兵，但是我知道，比起露营，她宁愿待在酒店。

今年6月，约塞米蒂及其周围地区的闪电天气导致公园里发生了九处火情。

露营河边

离到达公园还有大约一个小时左右的路程，由于山上的火情，我们不得不绕

---

stereo *n.* 立体音响   penny *n.* （美）分

pillow *n.* 枕头   lightning *n.* 闪电

long *detour* because of a fire on ⁚ hill. There was a lot of smoke, and I saw a *helicopter* drop water on the fire.

Finally, we drove into Yosemite National Park. Nana *smirked* as we wound through, admiring the fauna and the lush, green natural surroundings. "Maybe this trip won't be so bad after all," she said—though the frown on her face told a different story.

At Housekeeping Camp, we stopped at the ranger's office to pick out our campsite. I think Nana was getting into the trip because she asked more questions than I did. Eventually, a ranger showed us where our campsite was *located* on a map—beside Merced River. Despite her grumbling, Nana seemed pleased to have a view of a rushing river nearby. Our site was beautiful and the sound of water—a sound I never heard back in the city—was so close I could

---

很远的路。那儿有很浓烈的烟雾，我看见一架直升机在向大火喷水。

最后，我们终于到达了约塞米蒂国家公园。我们绕了很远，祖母欣赏着动物区里的动物和青葱的自然环境，笑了。"或许这次旅行并不是那么坏，"她说道——但她皱着的眉头出卖了她。

在露营管理处，我们在守护员的办公室里挑选我们的露营地。我想祖母慢慢地喜欢上了这次旅行，因为她问的问题比我还多。最后，一个守护员终于在地图上指出了我们的露营地——在默塞德河边。尽管祖母还是有些怨言，但是她似乎对附近可以看到河流很满意。我们的地点很漂亮，还有水声——我在城里从来没听到过——声音如此近，我几乎都能触碰到。

---

detour *n.* 绕道

smirk *v.* 得意地笑

helicopter *n.* 直升机

locate *v.* 确定……的位置

almost touch it. I wondered if it was the same view John Muir might have had years before.

Nana especially liked that we had a tent cabin rather than a plain tent and that we didn't have to sleep on the ground. Instead, the cabin had a *bunk bed*.

Nana and I built a *campfire* using some small *kindling* and newspaper she had brought along. We roasted hot dogs and covered them in mustard, and for dessert, we roasted *marshmallows*.

After dinner, Nana and I sat by the fire, planning the next day. I told her that I needed to get started on earning my Junior Ranger badge. Now that she was here, I think Nana wanted to help preserve Yosemite as much as I did!

The next morning, I looked through my *Junior Ranger Handbook*

我想这会不会与约翰·缪尔若干年前看到的是同一片景色。

祖母特别满意我们没有睡在布搭帐篷里，而是有一个帐篷小屋。因为有小屋我们就不用躺在地上了，而且小屋里还有个双层床。

我和祖母用了她带来的一些引火的东西和报纸生起了篝火。我们烤了几根热狗，在上面涂了些芥末，最后烤了点棉花糖当甜点。

晚餐之后，我们坐在火堆旁，计划明天的行程。我告诉她，我要开始夺取臂章的事业了。既然祖母已经到这儿来了，我想她应该和我一样，一心想要为保护约塞米蒂做些什么！

第二天一早，我在浏览我的《少年守护员手册》，祖母在一旁伸展她

---

bunk bed　双层床　　　　　　　　　　　campfire　n.　篝火
kindling　n.　引火的东西　　　　　　　　marshmallow　n.　棉花糖

as Nana *stretched* what she called her "aching feet." I thought it was pretty funny, since she walked miles every day in the city, but suddenly setting up camp and sleeping on a bunk bed had her feeling *grouchy* and sore.

As for myself, I needed to complete five activities to earn my badge, but the good news was that the word find and bear poster I did at home—luckily I'd brought them along—counted. That left only three more activities, and the badge would be mine!

Through the Woods

I asked Nana if she would help me, and she said she would. I hoped it would take her mind off her complaining.

Together we looked at the list of programs being offered in the daily camp *newsletter*, Yosemite Today. We found a Junior Ranger

---

的"痛脚"。我觉得非常搞笑,因为她每天在城里得走好几里路都不会怎么样,但是突然的露营,睡在双层床上却使得她的脚又酸又痛。

至于我自己,我得完成五项任务才能获得臂章,但是好消息就是:我在家查的字数以及做的黑熊海报——还好我带来了——可以算两项任务。那么只需要再做三项任务,臂章就是我的了!

穿越森林

我问祖母她是否愿意帮助我,她说她愿意。我希望这样她就不会再抱怨了。

我们一起看到露营地每日的时事通讯——今日约塞米蒂——上面有

---

stretch *v.* 伸展   grouchy *adj.* 爱抱怨的
newsletter *v.* 时事通讯

program being offered at 3:00 that afternoon at Happy Isles Nature Center.

With that settled, Nana helped me make a *checklist*: Word count? Check. Bear poster? Check. Happy Isles? Check. That left only two activities to do! I wasn't too worried about *running out of* choices because there were 14 activities listed in the handbook.

As Nana and I *considered* our many options, I wondered what John Muir might have picked because several of them seemed to be his specialty. Luckily, they looked like things I might be interested in doing as well.

Activity 7 was about the giant *sequoias*, which were by the Wawona Hotel, a place Nana wanted to visit.

Activity 9 was about the Ah-wah-nee-chee Indians. That activity

---

一连串任务，今天下午三点钟在开心岛自然中心有一个"少年守护员计划。"

待开心岛确定下来之后，祖母便给我做了一个清单：查数字？完成。黑熊海报？完成。开心岛？完成。最后只剩下两项任务了！我并不担心会没有选择，因为手册上有14种任务。

我和祖母考虑了许多选择，我在想约翰·缪尔可能会选择哪些任务，因为有一些任务似乎他相当擅长。幸运的是，这些也是我感兴趣的。

任务七是关于那棵巨大的美洲红杉，它在瓦沃纳酒店附近，而瓦沃纳是祖母很想去参观的地方。

任务九是关于阿瓦尼奇印第安人，这项任务看起来很有前途。因为第

---

checklist *n.* 清单   run out of 没有

consider *v.* 考虑   sequoia *n.* 红杉

looked promising. For one thing, the Indian Village of Ahwahnee was very close to where we were camping, and for another thing, I'd always been interested in Native Americans and how they lived. The real clincher was that Nana seemed eager to tag along. After shaking hands on it, Nana and I decided we would begin by going there.

This giant sequoia, called the Wawona Tunnel Tree, had a path cut 8 feet wide and 26 feet long for visitors to travel through.

A building from the Indian village of Ahwahnee

We went to the Indian Village and took the *self-guided* tour. We learned a lot as we walked from *displays* to *replica* buildings.

The Indians called their valley Ahwahnee, which means "valley with the gaping mouth" and called themselves the Ah-wah-nee-chee, which means "*dwellers* in Ahwahnee."

一，阿瓦尼印第安人村庄离我们露营的地方特别近；第二，我一直都对美国土著人以及他们的生活很感兴趣。关键是祖母似乎很想去。在达成一致之后，我们决定首先去那儿。

这棵巨大的美洲红杉叫作瓦沃纳隧道树，树根部有一条8英尺宽，26英尺长的通道可供游客穿越。

阿瓦尼印第安人村庄中的建筑

到达印第安人村庄之后，我们便开始自助游。我们一路看到了不少展品，还有仿造的建筑，学到了很多东西。

印第安人将他们的峡谷称作"阿瓦尼"，意思是"多洞穴的峡谷"，将他们自己称作"阿瓦尼奇"，意思是"阿瓦尼的居住者"。

---

self-guided *adj.* 自助的

replica *n.* 复制品

display *n.* 展品

dweller *n.* 居住者

During the cold winters, the Ah-wah-nee-chee traveled to the *foothills* where the climate was milder. In the spring, they returned to the High Sierra and Yosemite.

They found food that included leaves, stems, seeds, *bulbs*, and berries. Black oak *acorns* also made up a big part of their diet.

"I guess they didn't have fast food and pizza," I said as we learned more about their diet.

"No," Nana agreed, "but they sure had the right idea. I bet they had a lot less problems with their health than your old Nana does!"

After we finished the tour, Nana and I looked at my handbook again—only two activities to do before I got my badge!

在寒冬，阿瓦尼奇人就迁移到山脚，那儿的气候比较温和。到了春天，他们就回到高高的山脊和约塞米蒂。

他们发现的食物包括叶子、茎干、种子、球茎以及浆果。黑橡树果也是他们的食物中很重要的一部分。

"我想他们应该没吃过快餐和比萨饼，" 我在知道了他们的饮食情况之后说道。

"是啊，"祖母说，"但是他们的做法肯定是对的，我打赌他们肯定不像你的老祖母身体这么差！"

这一段旅行结束之后，我和祖母又看了一下手册——再完成两个任务就可以得到臂章了！

---

foothill *n.* 山脚   bulb *n.* 球茎
acorn *n.* 橡树果

We took the shuttle to Happy Isles Nature Center, where there were four trails teaching about the area's four different *environments*: forest, river, talus, and fen.

A park ranger took us on the talus trail. We had no idea what "talus" was but soon found out that talus is made up of the rocks that pile up at the bottom of a cliff from rock falls.

Rock falls are often caused by roots that can grow through the cracks in rocks and cause them to break loose.

Earthquakes, rainstorms, and *snowmelt* also can cause rocks to split and tumble down *mountainsides*.

Wow! So many natural forces are responsible for changing Earth's surface.

我们便乘车回到开心岛自然中心，那里有四条小路通往此地四种不同的环境：森林、河流、碎石麓积以及沼地。

一位公园守护者带领我们去了碎石麓积那条路。我们并不知道"碎石麓积"是什么，但是马上就知道了，碎石麓积就是由从山麓落下来的石头堆积在底部而形成的石头坡。

由于植物的根在石头的裂缝中也能生长，使得石头碎裂松弛，从而导致碎石下落。

地震、暴风雨以及融化的雪水也能导致石头的碎裂，滚落至山腰。

哇！如此多的自然力量都能导致地球表面的变化。

---

environment *n.* 环境　　　　　　　　　　earthquake *n.* 地震
snowmelt *n.* 融雪水　　　　　　　　　　mountainside *n.* 山腰

To Grandmother's Hotel We Go

That evening, since Nana had been such a great sport, we decided to pack up our campsite and spend a night at the Wawona Hotel.

Not only would Nana get a good night sleep and not wake up so *cranky*, we would be closer to the giant sequoias in the morning.

The Wawona Hotel has been helping guests in Yosemite since the late 1870s.

It was tough to leave the *peaceful* water, but the hotel turned out to be equally stunning. There were six white buildings with wide porches and *verandas* with vines growing on them and a *fountain* of

---

出发去瓦沃纳酒店

那天晚上，祖母体力很好，我们决定打包行李，去瓦沃纳酒店住一晚。

这样，祖母可以好好地睡一觉，醒来时不会觉得烦躁，而且我们一大早就离美洲巨红杉很近了。

瓦沃纳酒店从十九世纪七十年代末开始，就一直在为来约塞米蒂的旅客提供帮助。

离开这平静的河水挺不舍的，但是后来发现酒店也同样令人赞叹。酒店

---

cranky *adj.* 烦躁的　　　　　　　peaceful *adj.* 平静的
veranda *n.* 阳台　　　　　　　　fountain *n.* 喷泉

flowing water in the center of the *courtyard*. It was quite a *contrast* to where we stayed the night before.

After breakfast, we packed the car and headed to the Mariposa Grove of Big Trees. Once there, I would complete my last activity by wandering among the giant sequoias.

We took the shuttle to the Mariposa Grove, and from there, we took the tram ride to see and hear about the "Big Trees."

The Ah-wah-nee-chee's word for big trees was "Wah-wo-nah." We learned that there are almost 500 giant sequoias and some of them have been alive for almost 2,000 years.

The tram stopped at the Grizzly Giant, which is *estimated* to be about 1,800 years old, just over 200 feet tall, and has a trunk with a *diameter* nearly 30 feet.

一共有六栋白色建筑，里面的走廊和阳台很宽阔，上面还有藤蔓缠绕。院子中间有个活水喷泉。这番景象与我们前一晚待的地方形成了鲜明的对比。

早饭过后，我们收拾好车，便驶向马利波萨大树林。到达那儿之后，我就能参观大美洲巨红杉，然后完成我最后一项任务了。

我们在马利波萨树林里乘坐了电车，方便观察"大树"。

阿瓦尼称大树为"瓦沃纳"。我们发现大约有500课美洲巨红杉，一些已经存活了大概2000年。

电车停在了大灰树下，据估计它已经活了大约1800年了，200多英尺高，树干的直径差不多30英尺。

---

courtyard *n.* 院子　　　　　　　　　　　contrast *n.* 对比
estimate *v.* 估计　　　　　　　　　　　diameter *n.* 直径

It was so amazing to look up, ant-like, at the base of these towering, *magnificent* trees. Even Nana couldn't help but gaze, ever upward, as the trees disappeared into the hazy *thick* clouds above.

On the way out of Yosemite, I handed my book to a Ranger so that she could sign-off on the activities I completed. She, in turn, handed me a trash bag. She said that my last task was to collect a bag of trash because rangers always leave a place better than they had found it.

After a short time, picking up the candy and gum wrappers that tourists sadly leave behind, I returned to the Ranger's station.

She thanked me and then had me *recite* the Junior Ranger *oath*.

从这些耸立着的大树底下像蚂蚁一样往上看的感觉太妙不可言了。连祖母都情不自禁地凝视着大树，一点点向上看，直到看见大树都消失在厚厚的云层里。

从约塞米蒂出来的时候，我把手册交给了一个守护员，让她在我完成的任务上做记号。她给我一个垃圾袋，告诉我，我最后的任务就是捡一袋垃圾，因为守护员总是在要离开一个地方时使它比最初发现时更好。

不一会儿，我就捡了很多游客乱扔的糖纸和口香糖包装纸，然后我回到了守护员办公室。

她表示感谢之后，让我背诵了少年守护员誓词。

---

magnificent *adj.* 巨大的
recite *v.* 背诵

thick *adj.* 厚的
oath *n.* 誓词

The Patch, One of Many

I said proudly, "As a Yosemite Junior Ranger, I promise to do all that I can to help protect the animals, birds, trees, flowers and other living things, the scenery, and the other special *qualities* and places in Yosemite National Park. I will continue to learn about the nature and the history of the park even after I leave Yosemite."

The park ranger signed my handbook and handed me my first Junior Ranger patch. The patch was so cool—brown and shaped like an *arrowhead* with a big bear paw right *underneath* the words "Junior Ranger Yosemite." I was so proud, and Nana gave me a big smile.

During the long drive back through Yosemite National Park, Nana

---

臂章之旅，刚刚启程

我自豪地说："作为一个约塞米蒂少年守护员，我宣誓，我将竭尽所能去保护动物、鸟类、花草树木以及其他生物和景色，以及约塞米蒂国家公园的其他优质资源及景区。即使在离开约塞米蒂之后，我也会继续学习有关国家公园的环境与历史。"

守护员在我的手册上签了字，然后给我一枚臂章，这枚臂章相当酷——整体呈褐色，箭头型，在"少年守护者·约塞米蒂"字样下面还有一个大大的熊掌。我非常自豪，祖母也看着我开心地笑了。

在从约塞米蒂驾车回家的漫长旅程中，我们停下来很多次，拍了很多

---

quality *n.* 优质；高级　　　　　　　　　　　　arrowhead *n.* 箭头
underneath *prep.* 在……下面

and I stopped many more times to take photos. We were both sad to leave, even Nana, but to cheer me up Nana handed me a long list of national parks where I could earn more Junior Ranger patches. She said I needed to decide where we—that's right, "we"—could drive next summer and then to *circle* the ones I wanted to visit. There are so many. How will I ever choose? I asked Nana to help, and she was more than happy to do so. I think she has finally gotten over the fear of the outdoors. John Muir would be proud of both of us.

照片。我们都因为要离开而很难过，即使是祖母这会儿也情绪低落。为了使我开心起来，她给了我一个长长的国家公园清单，我可以从那获取更多的臂章。她告诉我，我得决定我们——是的，没错，"我们"——明年夏天去哪儿，然后圈出我想去的地方。这么多选择，我该选哪个呢？我寻求祖母的帮助，她也相当乐意。我想她终于克服了对户外的恐惧。约翰·缪尔会为我们俩而自豪。

---

circle *v.* 在……上画圈；将……圈起来

5

The Eruption of Mount Shasta

Chapter One

It is four o'clock in the morning, and Kyle Strong is sleeping. Oz, his dog, is curled up at the foot of his bed. Oz's tail is wagging a bit and his legs are twitching, which means he is dreaming about chasing rabbits again. Kyle is dreaming, too, but his dream is about changing into a *werewolf* while standing in front of his class giving a speech about George Washington. Kyle doesn't like this dream.

沙斯塔峰的喷发

第一章

现在是清晨四点钟，凯尔·斯特朗还在睡觉。他的狗奥兹正蜷缩在他的脚下。它摆动着尾巴，双腿也颤抖着，这意味着它又梦到追小兔子了。凯尔也在做梦，但是他的梦的内容是，在他当着全班同学的面做关于乔治·华盛顿的演讲的时候，变身为了狼人。凯尔不喜欢这个梦。

---

eruption *n.* 喷发   werewolf *n.* 狼人

In the corner of the room, a large black bird sits in a nest built *snugly* in the top shelf of a bookcase. The bird is a *crow*. But Kyle named him Raven, which has created a great deal of *confusion* for Raven. You see, throughout history, ravens have been seen as smarter, stronger, and wiser than crows. Crows have always aspired to be ravens. So Raven, being a crow, is more than a little confused. But not as confused as Kyle, who doesn't know a crow from a raven.

Kyle found Raven when he was still a baby. The mother crow had been killed by an *eagle* while protecting her nest. Raven was the only survivor. Kyle's dad caught the small bird and brought it home with them. After talking to some wildlife experts, they were given a permit to keep the crow as a pet.

在这个房间的角落，一只大黑鸟坐在笼子里，这笼子做得十分舒适，放置在书架最顶层的格子里。这是只乌鸦。但凯尔给它起名为"莱文"（意为"渡鸦"），这让莱文很是不解。纵观历史不难发现，渡鸦都要比乌鸦更加聪明，更强壮而富有智慧。乌鸦们都很向往能成为渡鸦。所以这让本来是只乌鸦的莱文满腹困惑。但凯尔一点也不困惑，因为他区别不了渡鸦和乌鸦。

凯尔发现莱文的时候它还是个小宝宝。莱文妈妈为了保护巢穴被老鹰杀害了。莱文是唯一的幸存者。凯尔的爸爸抓住了这只小鸟并且带回了家。他们与很多野生动物专家会谈后，才得到了将这只乌鸦作为宠物来养的许可。

---

snugly *adv.* 温暖舒适地

confusion *n.* 困惑

crow *n.* 乌鸦

eagle *n.* 鹰

So, where was I? Oh yes, four o'clock in the morning and everyone is sleeping. Mostly, this is just like any other night. Some sleeping, some *snoring*, a little dreaming, nothing out of the *ordinary*. So, what follows is a surprise—a surprise that was getting a little too common during the last few weeks.

The shaking is mild at first, and Raven opens one eye to see what is happening. Quickly, though, the slight shaking becomes a full earthquake, with things bouncing on the floor, books falling from shelves, and a window shattering from its pane. Kyle jumps from his bed, opens the window to let Raven outside, and takes Oz *downstairs*.

那么我在哪里呢？是的啊，清晨四点每个人都沉浸在梦乡之中。这只是一个很普通的夜晚。有的人在沉睡，有的人在打鼾，做点小梦，没什么特别的。所以，接下来发生的就有点让人震惊了——但这件令人震惊的事情在过去的几个星期里，好像显得再普通不过了。

最开始的时候震感并不明显，莱文睁开了一只眼睛想看看发生了什么事情。很快，这种轻微的震颤变成了真实的地震。东西都掉在了地上，书也从书架上掉了下来，窗子都震碎了。凯尔从床上一下子跳了下来，打开窗户让莱文飞出去，他带着奥兹下楼。

---

snore *v.* 打鼾   ordinary *n.* 普通
downstairs *adv.* 在楼下；往楼下

Kyle can barely keep his *balance* as he runs. The coat rack falls across the bottom of the stairs, so he and Oz jump over it and the pile of jackets. Kyle slips and falls, but he is not hurt. They make it downstairs just as the shaking stops.

His younger sister, Janet, and his parents are already downstairs standing in the main *entrance*, where the ceiling beams are the strongest.

"Is everyone okay?" Kyle's mom asks. Her voice is shaky, and she is holding onto Kyle's father. Kyle's father reaches out and pulls the whole family into his arms—everyone *except* Oz. Poor Oz always feels left out. He sneaks into the tangle of feet and rubs against any leg that is near him. He is scared, too, and wants to feel safe and loved like everyone else.

凯尔在跑的时候几乎不能保持平衡，衣架横在了楼梯底部，他和奥兹从衣架和一堆来克上跳了过去。凯尔滑倒了，但没有受伤。他们到达楼下的时候，震感停止了。

他的妹妹珍妮特和他的父母都站在大门那里，因为那里的房梁是最结实的。

"大家都没受伤吧？"凯尔的妈妈问道。她抱着凯尔的爸爸，声音都颤抖了。凯尔的爸爸伸出手将全家都揽进自己的怀里——除了奥兹的每一个人。可怜的奥兹总是有被遗忘的感觉。它钻进全家人的脚下，谁的腿离它近，它都要蹭上几下。它也同样害怕，它也需要安全感，需要像别人一样感受被爱。

---

balance *n.* 平衡　　　　　　　　　　　　　　　　entrance *n.* 入口
except *prep.* 除了

"Wow," says Kyle, "that was cool." He likes the excitement of an earthquake, but not until after it is over and he feels safe. "I'm going to call Justin." Kyle races back up to his room, with Oz close behind.

Chapter Two

Kyle dials Justin's phone number, but the line is busy, so he hangs up and tries again, getting through this time. "Hey, Justin, wasn't that cool?"

"I'm not Justin. Wait a minute, Runt, and I'll get him." Yuck! Justin's big sister, Amanda, answered. Kyle hates when she calls him "Runt." He's almost as tall as she is. He has mixed feelings about her. She can be *obnoxious*, but she is kind of cute.

"哇哦"，凯尔说，"真是酷啊。"他喜欢地震带来的刺激感，但是在他感到安全之前他并不喜欢这种刺激。"我去给贾斯汀打电话。"凯尔跑回了自己的房间，奥兹紧随其后。

第二章

凯尔拨通了贾斯汀的电话号码，但是线路忙，所以他挂断了重播，终于接通了。"嘿，贾斯汀，刚才真酷啊！"

"我不是贾斯汀，等一下，矮子，我去叫他。"啐！贾斯汀的姐姐阿曼达接的电话。凯尔很讨厌阿曼达叫他"矮子"。他们俩差不多一样高。他对她的感情很复杂。她有时候很讨人厌，有时候却很可爱。

---

obnoxious *adj.* 讨厌的

He kind of likes her, but she is three years older, and he never knows what to say around her.

"Hello?" Justin's voice is *quivering* a little, but he's trying not to sound scared.

"Hey, Justin, wasn't that cool? That's the fourth big earthquake this month. That's so cool." Kyle is still very excited and likes the feeling.

"Hey, Kyle. Yeah, that was cool," says Justin *unconvincingly*. "But, you know, the volcano guys on the news said that all these earthquakes might mean that Mount Shasta is getting active again. That's not so cool."

"Well, there must be plans for this sort of thing. It'll be cool. Even if Shasta *explodes*, it would be so rad to say we were there—that

---

他有点喜欢她，但是她比他大三岁，他永远不知道该跟她说点什么。

"喂？"贾斯汀的声音有点颤抖，但他尽量不暴露内心的恐惧。

"嘿，贾斯汀，刚才酷吧？那个是这个月以来第四次大地震，真是太酷了。"凯尔仍然很激动，他很喜欢这种感觉。

"嘿，凯尔。是啊，真是酷。"贾斯汀不太确信地说。"但是火山研究员在新闻上说，所有的这些地震可能预示着沙斯塔峰又再次活跃起来了。那可就糟了。"

"哦，对于这种事情一定会有应对策略的。还是很令人激动。即使沙斯塔峰喷发了，但我们能够目击现场真是太令人兴奋了！"凯尔仿佛看到

---

quiver *v.* 颤抖
explode *v.* 喷发

unconvincingly *adv.* 不确定地

we saw it explode." Kyle can see it in his head, a newsperson *interviewing* him about his experience. He can imagine his face on television and the fame he will have.

On the other hand, Justin imagines his house burning down and lava *destroying* the school. "Hey, wait," he thinks to himself, "no school. This might be cool after all." But instead he says to Kyle, "I'd rather say I saw it on the news, from far away."

Chapter Three

When he gets off the phone with Justin, Kyle begins to clean up his room. He puts the books back on the shelf and picks up the compact discs that are on the floor. His computer is not harmed, which is a *relief*.

了一个新闻记者在采访他，让他谈谈火山喷发的目击过程。他可以想象得到他的脸出现在电视机屏幕上和他即将拥有的声望。

可是贾斯汀想到的却是他们家的房子被烧毁了，火山岩浆毁了学校。"嘿，等一下，"他默默地想着，"毕竟没了学校还是好的。"但是他却对凯尔说，"我宁愿在新闻里看到这种场景发生在很遥远的地方。"

第三章

凯尔和贾斯汀通完电话，便开始打扫房间。他把书放回书架上，捡起地上的唱片。他的电脑完好无损，这让他松了一口气。

---

interview *v.* 采访　　　　　　　　　　　　destroy *v.* 毁坏
relief *n.* 放松

While Kyle cleans up his room, Raven flies up to the window and comes in through the cat door Kyle's dad *installed*. Having to use a cat door is another source of confusion for Raven, who would rather *tease* cats than use things created for cats. If he were human, Raven would be in *therapy*.

Kyle turns on the computer, logs onto the Web, and does a search for volcanoes. He finds a lot of information—so much that he feels overwhelmed by all the explanations. He turns on his radio and tunes it to the local news station to hear more about what happened. They are talking about the earthquake with some expert from San Francisco.

According to the guy on the news, Shasta City and the

当凯尔打扫房间的时候，莱文飞上窗户，从凯尔爸爸做的猫门进来了。出入要走猫门也让莱文困惑，它宁愿冒着生命危险去逗猫，也不愿屈尊使用给猫做的东西。如果莱文是人，一定会被送去医院看病。

凯尔打开电脑，登陆网站查找关于火山的信息。他找到了大量信息——所有的解释让他感到倍受打击。他打开收音机调到当地新闻，想了解更多的消息。新闻中，人们正和一位来自旧金山的教授探讨地震的事情。

根据新闻播报员的解说，沙斯塔城和所有沙斯塔峰周边的地区都处于黄色警戒的状态下。这也就意味着火山喷发是很有可能发生的，而且强度

---

install *v.* 安装　　　　　　　　　　　　　　　tease *v.* 嘲笑
therapy *n.* 治疗

surrounding areas at the base of Mount Shasta are in a Condition Yellow alert. This means there is some chance of an eruption and that it will be big enough to cause damage and *endanger* lives. Kyle hopes there isn't an eruption, fearing that these earthquakes are a little more serious than he had thought.

Kyle feels a little worried that something bad might happen, but the excitement is starting to wear off and he's tired. He can worry about it in the morning. "Good night, guys," he says, then turns out the light.

Chapter Four

Because of the Condition Yellow alert, school is *canceled* today, so Kyle plays video games with his sister, Janet.

绝对会造成毁坏和人员伤亡。凯尔希望火山不会喷发，他开始担心最近的几次地震比他想象中的严重许多。

凯尔对即将有可能发生的事情感到担心，那种兴奋感开始消失，他也累了。他可以明天再继续担心。"晚安，伙计们，"他说道，然后关了灯。

第四章

因为黄色警告，学校今天停课，所以凯尔和他的妹妹珍妮特玩起了电子游戏。

---

endanger *v.* 危害   cancel *v.* 取消

Later in the day, Justin comes over and they talk about how cool it would be if their school was buried by lava. Then they play video games.

In the video game they play, each person must *capture* many Samurai, then save a *princess* from an evil king. Meanwhile, an erupting volcano creates *hazards* to make their tasks more difficult. This is called *irony*.

Chapter Five

It is 1:00 on Sunday afternoon, three days after the last earthquake. Kyle is sitting on the couch watching a soccer game on television. Oz is curled up at his feet. Raven is on his perch in the kitchen, looking kind of nervous.

傍晚的时候，贾斯汀来到他们家，谈论起如果学校被火山浆埋起来了那该有多好。然后他们便一起玩电子游戏。

他们玩的游戏中，每个人必须俘虏很多勇士，然后从罪恶的国王手里解救公主。与此同时，火山喷发会加大游戏的难度。此刻玩这个游戏感觉真是讽刺。

第五章

现在是周日下午一点，距离最近发生的地震已有三天。凯尔坐在沙发上看着电视播的足球赛。奥兹在他的脚下蜷缩着。莱文站在厨房里它的栖木上，神色略有紧张。

---

capture *v.* 捕获　　　　　　　　　　princess *n.* 公主

hazard *n.* 困难　　　　　　　　　　irony *n.* 讽刺

Suddenly, the ground begins to shake and rumble. Mount Shasta is erupting. The explosion rocks the house, and it sounds like the whole world is being blown to bits. Kyle races to the window to look at the mountain, and what he sees sends chills through his whole body.

Above the mountain is an *enormous*, gray cloud of dust and ash spewing from the top of Mount Shasta. A *humongous* cloud is billowing upward like a giant *mushroom*. The ground is shaking, and the shaking gets worse with each passing second.

Kyle's legs feel weak and his knees are like rubber. His parents run into the room with Janet in his dad's arms. His mom is calm and *composed*, and she seems to be more in control of what needs to be done. Kyle looks to her for instructions.

突然，地面开始摇晃并发出隆隆声。沙斯塔峰开始喷发了。爆炸的力量使屋子震动起来，整个世界好像都要被炸成碎片。凯尔跑到窗户前看沙斯塔山，他看到的景象让他浑身战栗。

在山顶上方是一团巨大的包含着灰烬和尘土的灰色阴云，正从火山顶喷发出来。巨大无比的蘑菇云正如波浪般翻滚着汹涌向上。大地在颤动，震感每一秒都在加剧。

凯尔感觉腿发软无力，膝盖也如橡胶一般。他的父母冲进了房间，爸爸怀里抱着珍妮特。他的妈妈很淡定，似乎她对接下来要做的事情胸有成竹。凯尔看着她的妈妈，像是在问怎么办。

---

enormous *adj.* 巨大的   humongous *adj.* 巨大的
mushroom *n.* 蘑菇   composed *adj.* 镇定的

"Get your jacket—we have to leave, now. We don't have long." Her voice is firm and strong, but Kyle can still feel a hint of fear in it. As they gather their *belongings*, there is a pounding on the roof of the house. Small rocks and pieces of pumice are beginning to fall out of the exploding cloud of dust and ash.

Kyle's father herds everyone out the door. A rain of ash and dust is beginning to fall. Kyle's father works for the Forest Service, and he knows this is a bad sign. The situation is about to get very ugly. There is little time to waste.

"穿上衣服，我们现在就离开。没多少时间了。"她的声音坚定而富有力量，但是凯尔还是听出了一丝恐惧的意味。当他们收拾随身物品的时候，听到了屋顶上的重击声。那个巨大的云状物里满是灰烬和尘土，小石块和浮石开始从空中纷纷坠落。

凯尔的爸爸带着一家人逃离了这座房子。灰烬和尘土如同倾盆大雨从天而降。凯尔的爸爸在林业局工作，他知道这是一个很不好的征兆。情况将会变得更加糟糕，一秒钟都不能浪费了。

---

belongings *n.* 财产；携带物品

Just then, Kyle looks for Raven and Oz and doesn't see them. "Where's Raven? Where's Oz? We can't leave without them." Kyle is near tears.

"Come on, Kyle, we can't wait for the animals. They'll be okay." His dad doesn't think anything left behind is going to be okay, but they have to leave right now. There is no time to look for the dog or the bird.

"I'm not leaving without Oz and Raven." Kyle struggles free from his mother's hand and runs toward the house.

Chapter Six

The eruption *continues*. The cloud of dust and gas has grown so large that it blocks the sun and leaves the whole area with the

---

此时，凯尔到处找莱文和奥兹，却怎么也找不到。"莱文在哪里？奥兹在哪里？我们不能扔下它们不管。"凯尔快急哭了。

"过来，凯尔！我们不能再等它们了，它们不会有事的。"凯尔的爸爸并不是真的觉得它们会没事，但是他们现在必须离开。根本没有时间找狗和鸟。

"找不到莱文和奥兹我是不会离开的！"凯尔挣脱了他妈妈的手，冲向屋子。

第六章

火山继续喷发着。那团混杂着灰烬和尘土的云彩变得巨大，挡住了阳

---

continue *v.* 继续

shadowy feeling of a *nightmare*. A bright red glow appears around the top of the mountain from the lava pouring out of the throat of the volcano. The heat is melting the glacier that keeps Shasta crowned in ice year round. An avalanche of water and mud is flowing down the mountain, headed for several towns at the base of the mountain.

Oz and Raven are Kyle's best friends in the world. He can't imagine living without them. Oz was born in the same month as Kyle, and they have grown up together. And Kyle thinks of Raven as almost human. The thought of leaving him to fend for himself in the thick cloud of dust and ash is *unthinkable*.

Pieces of pumice are bouncing off of Kyle's head as he runs toward the house, but they are light. They sting as they hit, but they

---

光，阴影笼罩了大地，好似一场噩梦。一片亮红色出现在火山顶端，火山岩浆从火山喉部喷发出来。这种高温融化了常年覆盖在火山顶部的冰川。雪崩般的水流和泥浆从火山上冲了下来，冲向山脚下的城镇。

奥兹和莱文是凯尔在这世界上最好的朋友。他无法想象没有它们的日子。奥兹和凯尔出生在同一个月份，他们一起长大。凯尔认为莱文是最像人类的，要让它独自面对那么厚重的尘土云团是无法想象的。

当凯尔冲进房子的时候，浮石落到了他的头上，但是浮石很轻。被它们砸到的时候就像是被蚊子叮了一下而已，根本不痛。凯尔可以听到父母

---

shadowy *adj.* 阴影的
unthinkable *adj.* 难以想象的

nightmare *n.* 噩梦

don't hurt all that much. Kyle can hear his parents imploring him to turn around, but he *refuses* to leave without Oz and Raven.

Kyle hears Raven cawing off to his side, flying alongside him as he runs. "Find Oz, Raven—find Oz." The crow flies higher into the sky, risking his own injuries from falling rocks. After a moment, he swoops back down and flies beneath the tree line, as though he wants Kyle to follow him.

Kyle follows Raven down the street, and after a few moments Kyle realizes they are heading toward an old barn where Kyle and Justin have a clubhouse. They hang out there all the time with Oz and Raven. In the confusion, Oz must have run to the old hangout, a place where he always felt safe. Kyle realizes that Oz must be *disoriented* and just as afraid as he is.

恳求他出来，但是没有奥兹和莱文他是不会独自离开的。

凯尔听到莱文叫着朝他飞过来，飞着跟随在凯尔旁边。"找到奥兹，莱文——找奥兹。"这只乌鸦冒着被落石砸伤的危险飞向了高空。过了一会，它猛扑回来飞在树林线以下，好像是想让凯尔跟着他。

凯尔跟着莱文跑向了街道，过了一会凯尔意识到他们是在前往一个旧谷仓，那是他和贾斯汀的俱乐部。他们总是和莱文、奥兹在那里玩耍。奥兹一定是在慌乱之中跑回那里去了，那个总是让它觉得安全的地方。凯尔意识到奥兹一定是混乱极了，并且和他一样害怕。

---

refuse *v.* 拒绝   disorient *adj.* 分不清方向的

The rain of dust and ash is getting thicker, with almost six inches of gray stuff on the ground. Kyle keeps running, trying to stay beneath the trees as much as possible. Raven circles back and waits for him, then continues to lead the way.

When they reach the clubhouse, Oz is clawing at the front door, trying to get inside. As he scratches at the door, he is barking and whining. Kyle sees him and is relieved that his friend is okay. "Come here, Oz, come to me." Recognizing a *familiar* voice, Oz comes running, still barking and whimpering. "For a big German *shepherd*, you sure are a coward. Come on, boy, let's get out of here."

尘土灰烬落下来得越来越密集，在地面上已经有六英寸厚的灰色物质了。凯尔还在跑着，他尽量在树下跑，莱文盘旋一圈回来等着他，然后继续带路。

当他们到达俱乐部的时候，奥兹正抓着前门试图进去。它边抓着门还边哀嚎着。凯尔看到它终于松了一口气，他的朋友是安全的。"过来奥兹；到我这来。"听到了这个熟悉的声音，奥兹跑了过来但还是不停地哼哼着。"你看起来是个大个德国牧羊犬，但胆子可真小。过来吧伙计，我们离开这里。"

---

familiar *adj.* 熟悉的　　　　　　　　　　shepherd *n.* 牧羊犬

Chapter Seven

Larger chunks of pumice are now raining down on Shasta City. The eruption is still getting more violent, with more lava spewing from the crater. An avalanche of mud and ice is racing down the western slope of the mountain, leveling everything in its path. The hot wind *generated* by the volcano's *intense* heat has flattened a whole section of forest. Trees topple like *dominoes*.

The size of the cloud over the land far from the mountain has reached a critical mass, and it can no longer continue to expand. The *collapse* that follows will wipe out everything in its path. There will be no survivors; everything will be buried in ash exactly as it is.

Raven leads them back toward Kyle's house, where his parents are frantically awaiting his safe return. Janet is curled up in the back seat of the car oblivious to what is going on.

第七章

更大块的浮石降落在沙斯塔城。喷发变得越来越猛烈，越来越多的火山岩浆从火山口喷涌出来，把一切事物都阻隔在了半路上。由火山的高温引起的热风将一整片森林都刮倒了。树木像多米诺骨牌一样连续倒下。

离山很远的地面上方的云彩已经巨大无比，不能再看着它蔓延了。倒塌了的话将会卷起路上所有的东西，没有人能幸存；所有的一切都将被灰尘掩埋，就像此刻眼前的悲剧一样。

莱文要将它们带回了凯尔的家，在家里凯尔的父母正心急如焚地等待着他安全归来。珍妮特蜷缩在车的后座上，全然不知发生了什么。

---

generate *v.* 产生　　　　　　　　**intense** *adj.* 强烈的；剧烈的

domino *n.* 多米诺骨牌　　　　　　**collapse** *n.* 倒塌

Kyle runs for his life, while large pieces of pumice rain down all around him. Oz is at his heels, and Raven is *dodging* chunks of *pumice* as his wings flap wildly. Another earthquake strikes. The quaking ground makes it impossible for Kyle to stay on his feet and he crashes to the ground. He falls hard and is stunned. As he lies there, a small tree *collapse* under the weight of the ash that has accumulated on its leaves and branches. The tree falls and partly covers Kyle in ash and broken branches, leaving him trapped and unable to pull himself loose.

"Oz, come here, boy. Go home, get Dad." Kyle tries to push Oz away and send him for help, but his friend is loyal and stays by his side. "Please, Oz, go get help. I'm stuck and I can't get out, and I

凯尔拼命地跑着，大块的浮石正像雨点一样落在他的周围。奥兹紧跟在他旁边，莱文拼命挥动着翅膀，躲避着打向它翅膀的大块浮石。另一场地震开始了，颤动的大地让凯尔根本无法站立起来，他摔倒在地。他摔得很重，好像摔得失去了意识。在他摔倒的地方，灰土越积越重，把一棵小树压倒了。倒下的小树使凯尔的部分身体被灰尘和树枝压着，他卡在那里，动弹不得。

"奥兹过来。伙计，回家去通知爸爸。"凯尔试图把奥兹推走寻求帮助，但是他的这位忠诚的朋友坚持待在他的身边。"快，奥兹，去求救！

---

dodge *v.* 躲   pumice *n.* 浮石
collapse *v.* 倒塌；塌下

think my leg is broken. Go get Dad."

Raven lands at Kyle's side and caws a couple of times. This is his chance, an *opportunity* for Raven to live up to his name. If he gets Kyle's dad, he will be able to prove his worth as a simple crow. Maybe he won't need therapy after all. Raven *takes off* and flies to get Kyle's dad.

Oz licks Kyle's face and barks, but there is no one left to hear him. Oz won't leave Kyle here alone, so he begins to pull some of the tree limbs off Kyle. But the large limbs are too difficult for Oz to move, and Kyle remains trapped.

Kyle is *suddenly* very afraid, and his whole body shakes. He tries to stop, but he is crying now, sobbing with fear. He doesn't want to

---

我被困住了不能动，腿好像也受伤了。去通知爸爸。"

莱文飞落在凯尔的身边，叫了几声。这是它的机会，让自己和名字真正匹配的机会。如果它去通知了凯尔的爸爸，它就证明了自己只是一只简单的乌鸦，根本不需要去医院看病。莱文飞去找凯尔的爸爸。

奥兹舔着凯尔的脸，哀嚎着，但没有谁会听到。奥兹不会把凯尔独自留在这里的，它开始将一些树枝从凯尔身上移开。但是树枝太大，奥兹无能为力，凯尔还是被困着。

凯尔突然开始害怕起来，他的全身都颤抖了。他根本控制不住自己的眼泪，充满恐惧地啜泣着。他不想死——不想死在这里，不想在这么年少

---

opportunity *n.* 机会   take off 离开
suddenly *adv.* 突然地

die—not here, not so young. Oz *licks* his face and whines, feeling Kyle's fear intermingled with his own.

Chapter Eight

Raven soon finds Kyle's family, and he caws for them to follow him. He takes off, then circles back to see if they are following. Suddenly, Kyle's mother *figures out* that Raven wants them to follow him. They head off in the direction that Raven is flying. In only a couple of minutes, they are at Kyle's side. Kyle's dad lifts the large branch from his legs. Kyle gets up and limps to the car with his dad's help.

Just as they reach the car, Kyle looks up as he hears an *incredibly* loud, *thunderous* crack and sees the ash cloud begin to collapse.

的时候死去。奥兹舔着他的脸，哀嚎着，感觉凯尔的恐惧和它自身的恐惧融合在了一起。

第八章

莱文很快找到了凯尔一家，它叫了几声让他们跟着它过来。它飞着，然后盘旋着看看凯尔家人是否跟它来了。突然，凯尔的妈妈明白了莱文的意思。他们朝莱文带领的方向奔去。不一会，他们就找到了凯尔。凯尔的爸爸将大树枝从凯尔的腿上移开。凯尔爬起来，在爸爸的搀扶下跛着脚走向车里。

他们刚到车边上，凯尔听到了震耳欲聋的爆裂声，一抬头看见那团灰

---

lick *v.* 舔
incredibly *adj.* 难以置信的

figure out 明白
thunderous *adj.* 震耳欲聋的

Millions and millions of tons of ash, dust, and pumice stone rain back down. Kyle's dad understands immediately what is happening and hurries everyone into the car.

"Come on, we have to get out of here. Everybody in the car—hurry." He is *frantically* trying to get everyone in the car and settled before the *surge* cloud can gather too much speed. Oz curls up between Kyle and Janet on the back seat, and Raven perches in the back of the SUV.

Kyle watches out the rear window as a *massive* cloud of ash and dust races down the valley toward the city. There is enough ash in the cloud to bury the *entire* city, and it seems to be moving faster than their car. Kyle's father tells everyone to make sure they are buckled in and says to hold on tight. He takes off like a race car

---

烬云开始破裂。数不尽的灰尘、浮石像雨点一样坠落下来。凯尔的爸爸立即明白了发生了什么，催促大家赶快上车。

"快！我们必须马上离开这里。大家快上车！快点！"他发疯似地催促着大家上车坐好，每耽搁一秒钟，那团巨大涌云的破坏力都会成倍增加。奥兹蜷缩在后座上，在凯尔和珍妮特中间，莱文栖息在这个多功能车的后边。

凯尔通过后挡风玻璃看到一个巨大的灰烬云正急速飘过山谷，进入市内。云朵里的灰烬足以埋没整个城镇，这朵云行进的速度好像比他们的车速还快！凯尔的爸爸告诉大家要确保系好安全带，抓紧把手。他像职业赛

---

frantically *adv.* 发疯地　　　　　　　　surge *n.* 汹涌；奔腾
massive *adj.* 巨大的　　　　　　　　　 entire *adj.* 整个的

driver as he tries to *outrun* the *descending* cloud of dust and ash.

Chapter Nine

Fallen trees, *abandoned* cars, and very large stones litter the road. The surge cloud is gaining on them. Kyle's dad heads straight for the freeway, driving over lawns and through fields.

Raven is in the back, wishing he had flown on his own. He can make much better time than any car. The cloud behind them looks closer. Still, Kyle's dad drives like crazy, racing toward the freeway. As they reach the outer edge of Shasta City, the surge cloud is gaining on them and about to overtake them. A few large rocks hit the roof of the SUV, and it sounds like someone is pounding on it with a *sledgehammer*.

车手一样飙着车，像是要超过那朵不断下降的由灰烬和尘埃组成的云团。

第九章

折断的树，废弃的车，挡在路中央的大石头。汹涌澎湃的云逼近他们。凯尔的爸爸开着车穿过草地和农田，径直向高速公路开去。

莱文在后面，更希望自己能够飞起来。它飞得比任何车都快。后面的云跟得更紧了。凯尔的爸爸仍然疯狂地开着车直冲向高速公路。当他们到达沙斯塔城边的时候，这朵云已经逼近他们，并要把他们吞没了。一些大的石块已经砸到了车上，听起来像是谁在用大锤子砸车一样。

---

outrun *v.* 超过
abandon *v.* 抛弃；遗弃

descending *adj.* 下降的
sledgehammer *n.* 锤子

Looking out of the windows, they see a gray cloud of dust and ash where they used to live. Lava is flooding down the side of the mountain and may soon reach the city. They have *escaped* and they are relieved—but sad, knowing their home is buried beneath mud and ash.

As stories of heroism *emerge*, Kyle is recognized for his bravery in saving his dog. Raven is also recognized for his role in the rescue *mission*. Kyle's wish to see himself on TV comes true. Camera crews and reporters gather around, eager to hear his story. The next day everyone reads about Kyle, Oz, and Raven, and they see them on TV. Kyle becomes worried that all the attention may go to Raven's head. Raven may begin to think he is as smart as a raven, *instead of* the crow he is. It could take years of therapy to get him back to his normal self.

他们向车窗外望去，看到一团灰烬云飘浮在他们住的地方。火山岩浆如洪水般的从山顶上喷涌出来，很快就到达了城镇。他们已经逃脱了，也终于松了一口气——但不幸的是，自己的家园被灰烬掩埋。

英雄的故事开始流传，凯尔勇敢救狗的事迹被宣扬开来。莱文也在救援中扮演了重要角色。凯尔希望看到自己上电视的梦想就要实现了。好多相机不停地拍着，记者们也围得水泄不通，他们急切地想知道他的故事。第二天所有人都知道了凯尔、奥兹和莱文，因为大家在电视上看到了报道。凯尔开始担心，是不是人们所有的注意力都会集中在莱文的聪明才智上。莱文开始相信，它和真正的渡鸦一样聪明，而不仅仅是一只乌鸦。看来要进行多年的治疗才能够让它恢复正常了。

---

escape *v.* 逃脱
mission *n.* 任务

emerge *v.* 出现
instead of 而不是

6

Chick-a-Dude

An *Unexpected* Guest

Ffffffft. Christine's mom struck the match and lit the kiln as the potters circled the furnace. They pictured the freshly sculpted beads, bowls, mugs, and vases waiting to bake on the kiln shelf at 2,000 degrees Fahrenheit. They imagined how the glaze would make each *earthenware* piece come alive in *brilliant*, shiny colors.

Since second grade, Christine Brice came to her mom's pottery studio on Fridays after school. Christine's mom created *unique* clay

---

鸟兄

不速之客

咻。克莉丝汀的妈妈划火柴点着了炉子，陶艺师们都聚到炉前来。他们带着最新雕刻的珠子、碗、水壶和花瓶，等着在这个2000华氏度（1093.3摄氏度）的炉架上烘烤。他们想象着每一件陶器在上釉后会是多么光彩照人，活灵活现。

克莉丝汀·布莱斯自从二年级起就在每周五放学后到妈妈开的陶艺工作室来。妈妈为珠宝首饰制作独特的粘土珠子，但是克莉丝汀对陶轮更感

---

unexpected *adj.* 未料到的
brilliant *adj.* 色彩艳丽的

earthenware *n.* 陶瓷
unique *adj.* 独特的

beads for jewelry, but Christine was more interested in the potter's wheel. So she learned to *sculpt* pottery from her mom's friend and business partner, Mrs. Rodriguez, who created earthenware bowls on a potter's wheel. Her mom said *apprenticing* under an expert was one of the best ways to learn a craft.

"Your vases are so unique, Christine," cooed Mrs. Rodriguez, wiping her clay-covered hands with a towel. "I bet they sell out at the craft fair."

"I'm just excited they're considered good enough to be entered in the community-wide fair!" *squealed* Christine.

"Shhhh! Do you hear that sound?" interrupted Mrs. Brice.

兴趣。所以她从妈妈的朋友罗德里格斯太太那里学习陶艺雕刻，罗德里格斯太太和妈妈也有生意往来，她用陶轮制作陶碗。妈妈说过，拜专家为师是学手艺的一条最佳途径。

"克莉丝汀，你的花瓶好特别啊，"罗德里格斯太太柔声道，边说边用毛巾擦掉手上的泥土。"我保证这些花瓶在手工艺品集市上会供不应求的。"

"要是能在我们社区的集市和别的产品拼一下，我就会激动得不得了了！"克莉丝汀尖叫道。

"嘘！听见什么声音没？"妈妈插话说。

---

sculpt *v.* 雕   apprentice *v.* 做学徒
squeal *v.* 尖叫

The potters froze everything except their eyes, which shot up to the *rafters*.

Chirp, chirp, chirp.

"Well, I'll be!" exclaimed Mrs. Rodriguez.

A baby robin struggled out of a dark corner. Scritch scratch. Scritch scratch. The chick walked shakily along the rafters—*unaware* that its life was in danger not only from the increasing heat, but also from an *accidental tumble* to the wooden planks below.

"It's too late to turn off the kiln!" panicked Mrs. Brice. "That chick will roast up there!"

这几位陶艺师一动不动，只有眼睛四处打量着，最后目光聚集到了炉子的木梁上。

啾啾，啾啾，啾啾。

"哦，我的天哪！"罗德里格斯太太惊叹道。

一只小知更鸟从一个黑暗的角落里挣扎了出来。呲嚓。呲嚓。小鸟在木梁上摇摇晃晃地走着——还不知道自己危在旦夕，因为炉子的温度越来越高，或者它只要脚下一滑就会跌到下面的木板上。

"现在关掉炉子来不及了！"布莱斯太太惊慌起来。"那个小家伙在那会被烤熟的！"

---

rafter *n.* 椽
accidental *adj.* 意外的

unaware *adj.* 无知觉的
tumble *n.* 摔倒

"Ladies, we've got to *rescue* that little fella!" said Mrs. Rodriguez, heading for the heavy, *metal* ladder. Single-handedly, she carried in and set up the 12-foot-ladder. Then, like a *firefighter* rescuing a kitten from a tree, she boldly *ascended* the enormous ladder while carrying an empty box. She managed to coax the chick toward the box with chirping noises. The potters gathered around when she and the chick safely reached the ground.

"Well, chick," said Mrs. Brice. "We saved you from roasting like a marshmallow, but now what?"

Welcome to Our Home

Smiling broadly, Christine rolled into the house holding the box on her lap.

"女士们，我们必须得救下那个小家伙！"罗德里格斯太太说着就去拿那个重重的金属梯子。她一只手就把这个长12英尺的梯子拿了进来，架在那里。然后，她就像从树上救小猫的消防员一样，勇敢地拿着一个空箱子爬到了长梯子的高处。罗德里格斯太太发出啾啾的声音，好让小鸟到箱子里来。等她和小鸟安全落地，陶艺师们都围了过来。

"好吧，小鸟，"布莱斯太太说道，"我们救了你的命，不然你就得烤得像棉花糖了。但是现在怎么办呢？"

欢迎入宅

克莉丝汀开心地笑着，拿着箱子贴在大腿上，跌跌撞撞地进了房间。

---

rescue *v.* 营救   metal *adj.* 金属的
firefighter *n.* 消防员   ascend *v.* 登上

"What's in the box?" asked Mr. Brice, his curiosity piqued, knowing the fired pottery wouldn't be ready until the next day. That was what *typically* made his daughter smile like a Cheshire cat.

"Yeah, what's in the box?" echoed Christine's brother, Rick.

The chick answered the question for both of them with a chirp like a high-pitched whistle.

Christine spoke a mile a minute as she described the rescue and how they waited for the mama bird to return. She explained how they waited and waited, but the chick's mother failed to appear, so Christine volunteered to care for the chick until it was strong enough to fly.

"箱子里是什么东西？"布莱斯先生好奇地问道，因为他知道烧制的陶具明天才能做好。而通常只有新一批陶具出炉，她女儿才会发出这种傻笑。

"对啊，箱子里是什么？"她弟弟里克也附和着问道。

这时小鸟又发出了啾啾的声音——就像尖声的口哨——把这两个人的问题都给出了答案。

克莉丝汀像发连珠炮似地讲述着营救小鸟，还有等待小鸟妈妈回来的过程。她说在场的几个人等了又等，但是小鸟的妈妈一直没回来，所以克莉丝汀自告奋勇照顾小鸟，等它长大些再放飞它。

---

typically *adv.* 代表性地；经典地

"Rick, would you grab the *aquarium* from the attic? I think it will be perfect," said Christine.

As Rick flew out of the kitchen, Misty entered. She slowly headed to the box—ears perked, tail stiff, hair up. Her nose twitched as rapidly as a *hummingbird's* wings—*furiously* sniffing the chick she couldn't see. Then she broke into a deep and angry bark.

"Uh-oh," said Christine, grabbing Misty's collar just in time. Misty obeyed commands most of the time, however, the *temptation* appeared to be too much for her training. She struggled against Christine's grip as Mrs. Brice and Rick transferred the chick from the box to the aquarium. Mrs. Brice cleared a high shelf in the kitchen for the chick's aquarium—safe from their 110-pound bounding Labrador

---

"里克，你去阁楼里把家里的鱼缸拿来好吗？正好可以把小鸟放进去。"克莉丝汀说。

里克飞奔出了厨房，米斯蒂进来了。她慢慢地走向那个盒子——只见她耳朵竖立，尾巴挺直，连毛都立起来了。她的鼻子闪电般地抽吸着——她还没看见小鸟，但嗅到了小鸟的气味就已经让她发狂。然后，她怒不可遏地发出了一声狂吠。

"哦，不会吧，"克莉丝汀及时地拉住了米斯蒂的项圈。米斯蒂平时非常听话，可是此刻面前强大的诱惑仿佛使所有的训练都前功尽弃了。看到布莱斯太太和里克将小鸟从箱子转到了鱼缸，它更是用尽力气要挣脱克莉丝汀的控制。布莱斯太太在厨房的一个高架子上清出来一块地方放置装

---

aquarium *n.* 鱼缸
furiously *adv.* 暴怒地

hummingbird *n.* 蜂鸟
temptation *n.* 诱惑

retriever, Misty. Mrs. Brice lined the aquarium with newspaper, placed a shallow dish of water in the corner, and folded one of Rick's soccer socks into a *cozy* nest.

When Rick asked what robin chicks eat, Mr. Brice grabbed a plastic cup and headed to the garage for *shovels* and flashlights. "Worms," he called over his shoulder. "Let's get digging, gang!"

"Chirp, chirp, chirp!" Christine *squeaked* as she dropped worms into the chick's gaping beak after her family's garden-digging adventure. She then helped her parents prepare the family's dinner. After their own stomachs were full, the Brices watched the chick gobble up more worms, then they all headed to bed.

小鸟的鱼缸——放高一点，让米斯蒂怎么跳也伤不到它，米斯蒂可是条重达110磅的拉布拉多巡回犬。布莱斯太太在鱼缸里垫了报纸，又在角落里用浅碟盛了水，最后用里克的一只运动袜给小鸟做了一个舒服的窝。

里克问小知更鸟都吃什么，布莱斯先生抓起一个塑料杯，带上铲子和手电筒向车库走去。"虫子，"他转头喊道，"我们去挖虫子吧，伙计们！"

"啾啾，啾啾，啾啾！"克莉丝汀边向小鸟张开的小嘴里喂虫子，边发出小鸟一样的尖叫声。她刚和家人在花园里挖虫归来，然后又帮爸爸妈妈准备晚饭。全家人吃饱饭，都来看着小鸟狼吞虎咽地吃下不少虫子，之后才去睡觉。

---

retriever *n.* 巡回犬

shovel *n.* 铲子

cozy *adj.* 舒适的

squeak *v.* 尖叫

Before crawling under the covers with her novel, Christine went online using her computer and Web browser and learned that *in addition to* worms, robins eat berries and fruit, such as grapes, cherries, and tomatoes.

At breakfast, Christine *mimicked* a mama bird by "chirp, chirp, chirping" as she dropped worms and grape halves into the chick's waiting beak. Over buckwheat waffles and *strawberries*, the family voted to name the chick Chick-a-Dude because, as Rick *commented*, "He looks like a cool dude when he sticks out his chest."

Wearing Out His Welcome

All morning, Chick-a-Dude looked to the nearest person for food whenever he heard, "Chirp, chirp, chirp." Everyone enjoyed the

---

克莉丝汀在爬进被子里看小说之前，又打开电脑上网浏览了一番，知道了知更鸟除了吃虫子，还吃浆果和水果，比如说葡萄、樱桃和西红柿。

吃早饭时，小鸟张开嘴巴等着美食，克莉丝汀则像小鸟妈妈一样发出"啾啾，啾啾"的声音来喂小鸟吃虫子和切开的葡萄粒。全家人吃过了荞麦华夫饼和草莓后，投票决定给这只小鸟起名叫"鸟兄"，因为里克描述它说："它昂首挺胸的样子真像是一位很酷的老兄。"

宠爱难留

每天早晨，鸟兄只要听见"啾啾，啾啾"的声音，就会看着离它最近的人，等着有人来喂食。全家都很喜欢这只毛茸茸的小鸟——当然，只

---

in addition to 除了
strawberry *n.* 草莓

mimick *v.* 模仿
comment *v.* 评论

fluffy chick—everyone, that is, except Misty, whose stress level had not *decreased* since the Brices took Chick-a-Dude into their home. That afternoon, while Christine wrote invitations in her bedroom for her upcoming birthday party, Misty sat beneath Chick-a-Dude's aquarium in the kitchen and stared at the unwelcome houseguest.

"WOOF! WOOF!"

A terrified Chick-a-Dude sprung into the air as though lifted like a puppet by a string and landed—plonk!—in an empty stew pot on the stovetop.

Christine heard the *commotion* and raced to the kitchen. "I think we need to get you to a safer place," she told Chick-a-Dude, "and give you your *territory* back," she told Misty.

有米斯蒂不喜欢它。自从鸟兄来到布莱斯家，米斯蒂的压力等级就只升不降。有天下午，克莉丝汀在卧室里写生日聚会的邀请函——马上就是她的生日了，米斯蒂坐在厨房里鸟兄的鱼缸下方，瞪着这位讨厌的来客。

"汪！汪！"

鸟兄吓得"飞"了起来，但它飞的姿势更像是被提线控制的木偶，然后直线坠落——砰！——鸟兄摔进了炉顶的一口空蒸锅里。

克莉丝汀听见外面的声响，冲到了厨房。"我们得给你找个安全点的地方了，"她对鸟兄说；"也得让你收复失地，"她又告诉米斯蒂。

---

decrease *v.* 下降   commotion *n.* 喧闹，骚乱
territory *n.* 领土

A Home of His Own

"You must be Christine and Chick-a-Dude," guessed a woman named Kay as they entered the yard gate. "We spoke on the phone. I'm so glad you found us on the Internet."

"My mom drove me right over after we spoke."

"You did the right thing by bringing Chick-a-Dude to the Wildlife Rescue Center," said Kay. "hundreds of species of injured or *orphaned* wildlife—*mammals*, birds, and reptiles—come through these doors, and our staff is trained to provide the best possible care for all of them."

Kay went on to explain that a *veterinarian* would examine Chick-a-Dude. Then, because Chick-a-Dude already had his flight feathers,

---

回归家园

"你一定是克莉丝汀，这位一定是鸟兄了，"克莉丝汀带着小鸟走进庭院时，一个叫凯伊的女子猜测道。"我们通过电话。很高兴你在网上联系到了我们。"

"我们一通完电话，妈妈就开车送我过来了。"

"你把鸟兄送来'野生动物救助中心'是正确的，"凯伊说，"有上百种受伤的，或是被抛弃的野生动物从这里得到了救助——有哺乳动物，有鸟类，也有爬行动物。我们的工作人员都受过专业训练，会给它们提供最佳的照顾。"

凯伊继续解释说，会有兽医为鸟兄做体检。因为鸟兄已经长出了飞羽，

---

orphan *v.* 使成为孤儿　　　　　　　　mammal *n.* 哺乳动物
veterinarian *n.* 兽医

he'd stay in the flight cage where he'd practice flying with other rescued birds. He'd be fed every 30 minutes by hand—food and *vitamins*. After two or three weeks of all this nurturing, he'd be *released* into the wild near other robins where he should *thrive*.

"What a relief!" said Christine, scooping pasta onto everyone's plate that evening. "Chick-a-Dude's going to be A-Okay."

"That chick was totally cool," added Rick. "I'll miss the little guy's 'chirp, chirp, chirping'."

"Grrrrrr WOOF!" Misty *growled* as she slept curled up on her pillow.

"Misty won't," giggled Mrs. Brice.

所以接下来它就可以进入飞行笼，在那可以和其他被救助的鸟一起练习飞行。每30分钟就会有专人喂食——有食品，还有维生素。这样饲养二到三周之后，就可以把它放飞到野外去，和其他的知更鸟一起，茁壮成长。

"真是松了口气！"克莉丝汀说。晚饭时她给家人都盛上了意大利面。"鸟兄会生活得很好的。"

"那个家伙真是太酷了，"里克说道，"我会想念它的叫声的，'啾啾，啾啾，啾啾'。"

"哼……汪！"米斯蒂狂吠了一声，本来它正在枕头上蜷着身子睡觉呢。

"米斯蒂可不想它，"布莱斯太太咯咯地笑着说。

---

vitamin *n.* 维生素　　　　　　　　　release *v.* 释放
thrive *v.* 茁壮成长　　　　　　　　　growl *v.* 狂吠

7

Bats in the Attic

Introduction

When I was nine years old, I spent the summer visiting my great-grandmother, whom I called Gram. She lived in a large gray cedar shakes house by the ocean. Gram let me pick which upstairs bedroom I wanted to stay in, so I chose the yellow one because its window faced the beach.

I had many *adventures* that summer, including ones with *horseshoe* crabs, *sandcastles*, and ants. My latest adventure began when I heard

阁楼里的蝙蝠

引子

我九岁那年和曾祖母一起度过了暑假，我叫她太姥姥。她住在海边一座有杉木房顶的灰色大房子里。太姥姥让我选一间我喜欢的楼上卧室，我选了那间黄色卧室，因为房间的窗户面向海滩。

那个暑假我有很多奇遇，包括救起马蹄蟹，建沙堡，平息蚂蚁之灾等。而最近的一次奇遇是从我听见卧室窗户外的奇怪声响开始的。我向窗

---

adventure *n.* 奇遇　　　　　　　　　　horseshoe *n.* 马掌；马蹄铁
sandcastle *n.* 沙堡

some strange sounds outside of my bedroom window. I looked out and saw winged creatures flying around the outside light. These brown, flying animals seemed to fly *back and forth* from the house. I thought Gram's house might have bats in the attic.

Research

I had never climbed up the steep stairs to the third floor, but Gram had told me it was her attic. The strange sounds outside made me *curious* about what was in that part of the house. I decided to tell Gram about the bats the next morning. I planned to ask her if Jim could go with me to see how the bats were getting into the house. Jim was Gram's friend who helped her with chores around the house. He often stopped by to visit.

The next morning, while having a breakfast of *oatmeal* with lots of

---

外看去，看到有东西挥着翅膀围绕外面的光飞来飞去。这些棕色的动物似乎在绕着房子循环往复地飞着。我猜想，太姥姥家的阁楼里可能有蝙蝠。

调查

我从来没有爬上家里陡峭的楼梯到三楼去过，但是太姥姥告诉过我，那一层是阁楼。外面的奇怪声响让我开始好奇阁楼里到底有什么。我决定，第二天早上就告诉太姥姥家里有蝙蝠的事。我要问问她，吉姆能不能和我一起去那看看蝙蝠是怎么进入房子里的。吉姆是太姥姥的朋友，经常帮她干活，也经常过来坐坐。

第二天的早饭是加了很多枫糖浆的麦片，吃饭的时候我对太姥姥提起

---

back and forth 来来回回　　　　　　　　curious *adj.* 好奇的
oatmeal *n.* 麦片

maple syrup, I told Gram what I had seen and heard the night before. Gram said she didn't think the bats were living in the attic but it would be a good idea to have Jim and me check it out the next time he came to visit. Gram *suggested* that I ride my bike to the library to read all I could about bats. I was surprised when she told me that she didn't want the bats to go away, but she didn't want them to live in her house either.

The town's library was small, and the librarian knew me from *previous* visits. That summer I had read books about sand castles, horseshoe crabs, and ants, as well as books about tides and the ocean. Now I wanted books about bats.

The librarian helped me find many books, and I sat down to look through them. Some books were too difficult, and some were

---

了我前一天晚上听到的声音。太姥姥说她觉得阁楼里应该不会有蝙蝠，但是她很赞成让吉姆下次来的时候和我一起去看看。太姥姥建议我骑车去图书馆尽量多了解有关蝙蝠的知识。听到她说不想赶走蝙蝠，我很是吃惊，但是她也说不希望蝙蝠住在自己的房子里。

镇上的图书馆很小，我之前去过几次，图书管理员已经认识我了。那年夏天，我读了关于沙堡、马蹄蟹和蚂蚁的书，也读了关于潮汐和海洋的书。现在我想读读关于蝙蝠的书。

图书管理员帮我找出了很多书，我坐下来每本浏览了一下。有些书内容太难，有些又太简单。我选了三本最适合我读的书，做了登记，然后就

---

suggest *v.* 建议   previous *adj.* 之前的

too easy. I found three books that I thought would teach me what I wanted to learn, checked them out, and rode my bicycle home.

Blind as a Bat?

Bats are very interesting creatures. I learned that they are *divided* into two *categories*: megabats and microbats. Megabats can have a *wingspan* of six feet. Thank goodness the bats at Gram's were microbats, which are about the size of a *hamster*. Megabats live where it is warm all year, and they eat mostly fruit and nectar. Microbats live in many parts of the world and eat mostly insects. I was pretty sure Gram's bats were called Eptesicus fuscus (ep-TEAS-ick-us FUSS-cus), or big brown bats. Once I read further, I learned one bat could eat 600 to 1,000 mosquito-sized insects in an hour. Now I knew why Gram wanted to keep them near.

骑车回家了。

　　盲如蝙蝠？

　　蝙蝠是很有趣的动物。我知道了蝙蝠共分为两类：巨蝠和微蝠。巨蝠的翼展可达6英尺。谢天谢地，在太姥姥家出现的蝙蝠是微蝠，它们的身材只有仓鼠那么大而已。巨蝠生活在常年温热的地方，它们的食物主要是水果和花蜜。而微蝠在世界很多地方都能见到，主食昆虫。我现在很确定太姥姥家出现的蝙蝠叫"大棕蝠"，也就是棕色的大蝙蝠。我接着读下去，知道了一只蝙蝠一小时能吃下600到1000只蚊子大小的昆虫。现在我明白太姥姥为什么想让这些蝙蝠留在家附近了。

---

divide *v.* 划分　　　　　　　　　　　category *n.* 类
wingspan *n.* 翼展　　　　　　　　　　hamster *n.* 仓鼠

I first *suspected* bats were related to mice, but I read that bats are more closely related to humans. A bat's wing is like a human hand with four fingers and a thumb. The bat's arm has a *forearm*, an elbow, and an upper arm. Bats' fingers are long and have a double layer of skin connecting them. The skin is so thin you can almost see through it. Bats feed milk to their *newborns*, called pups, the same way other mammals do. Bats, like all mammals, have hair or fur on their bodies, are warm blooded, and have claws or *fingernails*. It was strange to think of those flying reatures outside my bedroom window as mammals. Obviously they were not flying rats!

I had heard the expression "blind as a bat" used by many people. In my reading, I found out that bats are not blind. They use their eyesight during daylight and early evening hours. At night, of course,

---

　　我起初猜想蝙蝠和老鼠很像，但是从书里我知道了蝙蝠和人类的关系更紧密。蝙蝠的翅膀就像人类的手，有一个大拇指和四个其他的手指。蝙蝠的手臂包括前臂、手肘和上臂。蝙蝠的手指很长，每两个手指间由双层的皮肤连接着。蝙蝠皮肤很薄，薄到几乎透光。它们会给幼仔喂奶，这一点和其他的哺乳动物一样。和所有哺乳动物一样的还有，蝙蝠也有皮毛，是恒温动物，有爪或指甲。想到卧室窗外飞着的动物竟然是哺乳动物，真是觉得怪异。显然，它们并不是会飞的老鼠那么简单！

　　我曾听很多人用过"盲如蝙蝠"这个说法。但读完书，我发现蝙蝠并不是真的看不见。他们白天和夜幕刚降临的时候主要靠视觉。当然，晚上

---

suspect　*v.*　猜想
newborn　*n.*　幼仔

forearm　*n.*　前臂
fingernail　*n.*　指甲

they need more than sight to catch flying insects and to fly around without hurting themselves. They do this by using *echolocation*. A bat makes sounds from its mouth or nose that bounce off solid objects and echo back, which tells the bat the location of the object, including insects.

Searching for Bats

The next time Jim came for breakfast, I asked him if he'd go with me to look for bats in the attic. As we climbed the narrow, *steep* stairs, Jim told me not to touch any bats we found. I told him I had read that only a few bats have *rabies*, but humans still should not touch or frighten them. Jim was glad I had done some research. He said it was good we both knew what to do, and what not to do, to stay safe around wildlife.

它们要捉飞着的昆虫，还要四处飞又不伤到自己，光靠视力就不够了。它们使用的是"回声定位法"。蝙蝠用嘴或鼻子发出声音，声音在遇到实物后折回，形成回声，这样蝙蝠就知道昆虫等物体的位置了。

寻找蝙蝠

吉姆又过来吃早饭时，我请他和我一起去阁楼里看有没有蝙蝠。我们俩从狭窄、陡峭的楼梯向上走时，吉姆告诉我有蝙蝠的话也不要去碰。我告诉他，书上说只有少数蝙蝠携带狂犬病病毒，但是还是不应该接触或是惊吓蝙蝠。吉姆听到我早有准备，感到很高兴。他说我们都知道怎样行动就太好了，这样与野生动物共处时也能保证安全。

---

echolocation *n.* 回声定位　　　　　　　　　　steep *adj.* 陡峭的
rabies *n.* 狂犬病

The attic was full of old things, such as furniture, boxes, and old pictures. Jim shone a flashlight onto the ceiling, looking for bats. We also looked all over the floor for bat *droppings*. We found nothing. The bats had to be living in the walls.

In one of the books I had read, I learned how to remove bats from a house. The book said not to *disturb* bats during the summer months in case there were young pups that would not be able to follow their parents to a new home. Gram would have to wait a couple more weeks until September to take steps to protect her house against any more bats living in it. I gave her the book that explained how to keep bats out so she would know what to do.

I asked Jim to help me build a bat house. The bat house would attract bats so they would stay near Gram's house to eat *insects*.

阁楼里装满了旧物，有家具、盒子和旧照片。吉姆拿手电筒照在棚顶，看有没有蝙蝠。我们还仔细地在地上看了一下有没有蝙蝠的粪便。但我们什么都没有找到。蝙蝠一定是住在墙里面了。

我在一本书中读到过驱赶房中蝙蝠的方法。书中说，不要在夏季惊扰蝙蝠，否则可能会有蝙蝠幼仔被落下，不能一起搬到它们的新家。太姥姥得等上几周了，到了九月份就可以采取措施来防止蝙蝠来家里骚扰了。我把讲蝙蝠驱赶之法的那本书给了太姥姥，这样她就知道到时候怎么做了。

我让吉姆帮我为蝙蝠盖个窝，蝙蝠喜欢这个窝的话就会住在太姥姥家附近，把周围的昆虫吃掉了。这个蝙蝠窝就盖在太姥姥家屋顶旁边，也就

---

dropping *n.* 粪便

disturb *v.* 打扰

insect *n.* 昆虫

When we were finished, Jim *fastened* the bat house near the edge of Gram's roof where I had seen the bats coming and going at dusk. I hoped the bats would learn to live in the new home we made for them.

Clam Digging

My summer was coming to a close; Labor Day was just a week away. I loved living at the shore and was not ready to leave. I missed my family and friends in the city, but I wished we lived closer to Gram.

One evening, Jim and Gram told me they had a surprise for me. The next day we were going to go clam digging. There was a full moon that night, which meant the tide would *ebb*, or pull away from shore, farther than *usual*. In the morning we would be able to dig

---

是我黄昏时看见蝙蝠盘旋的地方。窝盖好以后，吉姆又加固了这个新窝。我希望这些蝙蝠会住在我们为它们盖起的新窝里。

挖蚌

我的暑假马上就结束了；再过一周就是劳动节了。我喜欢住在海滩边，还不想动身离开呢。我想念城里的家人和朋友们，要是我们家和太姥姥家住得近一点就好了。

一天晚上，吉姆和太姥姥说他们给我准备了一个惊喜。第二天，我们要去挖蚌。前一天晚上是满月，这就意味着海水会退潮，还会比平时退得更低。早上我们就可以去挖蚌，不退潮的时候蚌都埋在海里了。我们早上

---

fasten *v.* 加固　　　　　　　　　　　　　　　　ebb *v.* 退潮
usual *adj.* 通常的

clams that were normally covered by the ocean. We would need to leave Gram's house by 6 a.m.

Gram, Jim, and I had a quick breakfast of cereal and orange juice. We had a short drive to a *secluded* beach. When we arrived, Jim handed me a wire bucket and a jug of water. He carried a potato hoe that looked like a *rake* with six long tines, and a big iron kettle. Gram carried a blanket and a picnic basket.

Gram and Jim showed me which *dimples*, or holes in the sand, should yield clams. Jim would find a dimple, put the hoe on the ocean side of the clam and push down, *gently* bringing the sand out. It was my job to grab the clam and put it into the bucket.

Clams dug down deeper into the sand to escape, so sometimes

6点就要从太姥姥家出发。

我、太姥姥和吉姆飞快地吃了麦片，喝了橘汁，开车很快就到了一处僻静的海滩。我们到了以后，吉姆递给我一个金属桶和一大杯水。他带了一把挖土豆的锄头——锄头看起来就像有六个尖齿的耙子——还有一个大铁罐。太姥姥带了一个毯子和一个野餐篮子。

太姥姥和吉姆给我讲什么样的沙坑里会有蚌。吉姆能找到沙坑，他把锄头放在有蚌的海水中，再把锄头铲下去，轻轻地把沙子挖出来。我的任务就是抓住蚌，再放进桶里。

蚌会继续钻向沙子深处想要逃脱，所以有时吉姆就得一直挖。当我们

---

secluded *adj.* 僻静的
dimple *n.* 小坑

rake *n.* 锄头
gently *adv.* 轻轻地

Jim had to keep digging. Clams also defended themselves by shooting a stream of water out of the hole as we stepped near them.

After a while, Jim handed me the hoe to try clam digging. I could not dig fast enough at first, but when I *uncovered* my first clam I was high-fiving Gram and Jim with happiness! Gram would swoosh the bucket of clams in the ocean water to remove sand from their shells.

Sometimes sea gulls would see a clam's snout near the surface, grab it, and fly off with it for a meal. I shooed the gulls away when they came too near to our digging. Gram told me that we might dig up a few bloodworms, as their holes in the sand look very similar to clam holes. I was very glad we didn't find a *bloodworm* that day; they can give humans *nasty* bites.

接近蚌的时候，蚌还会从洞里喷出水柱进行自我防御。

过了一会，吉姆就把锄头给我，让我试着挖蚌。我最初挖得不够快，当我终于挖到了蚌时，我高兴地与太姥姥和吉姆击掌祝贺！太姥姥把装蚌的桶在海水里快速地涮一下，好冲掉蚌壳上的沙子。

有时，海鸥在海面看见蚌张开的口，就会抓住蚌，叼走做一顿美味。海鸥飞得离我们挖蚌的地方太近的时候，我就把海鸥赶开。太姥姥告诉我，我们也可能挖到红蚯蚓，因为沙子里的红蚯蚓洞和蚌洞看起来很像。我很高兴我们那天没挖到红蚯蚓，红蚯蚓会在人身上留下很恶心的咬痕。

---

uncover *v.* 发现　　　　　　　　　　　　bloodworm *n.* 红蚯蚓
nasty *adj.* 恶心的

Bon Appétit!

Once we had collected quite a few clams, Gram and I looked for *driftwood*. We were at a *private* beach where we were allowed to build a fire. When we had our arms full of all sizes of wood, we headed back to Jim. He had the bucketful of clams and was washing the last ones in the ocean. Gram put the clams into her kettle and poured the jug of water over them to *remove* as much sand as possible. Jim built the fire, poured the water off the clams, and set the kettle atop the fire to cook. As the clams steamed, Gram sat on the blanket watching Jim and me make a sand castle.

Gram called us when the clams opened their shells. She put some salt, pepper, and butter on them. They were a grayish color when we dug them. Now cooked, they were almost white. Gram put

祝你好胃口！

我们挖到了很多蚌之后，我和太姥姥就找起浮木来。我们所在的是个私人海滩，这里允许生火。我们俩双手抱满大大小小的木头，回来找吉姆。我们到那里时，吉姆拿着装满蚌的小桶，正在海水里清洗最后几个蚌。太姥姥把蚌放进罐子里，又用大水壶向罐子里倒水，尽量把沙子都冲洗出去。吉姆生起火，又在装蚌的罐子里倒满水，最后把罐子放在火上煮起来。蚌在加热时，太姥姥坐在毯子上，看着我和吉姆盖沙堡。

当蚌的壳打开之后，太姥姥叫我们俩过去，她在蚌上洒了一些盐、辣椒粉和奶油。我们挖蚌的时候，蚌是灰颜色的。煮熟了以后，蚌变成了几

driftwood *n.* 浮木　　　　　　　　　　private *adj.* 私人的
remove *v.* 移动

one on a plate and showed me how to remove the skin on the snout. Then she gave it to me to eat.

"Bon appétit," said Jim. "Enjoy!"

The clams were *delicious*. With fresh bread and ice-cold *lemonade*, this was the best meal I had ever tasted.

Goodbyes

Gram, Jim, and I went for a long walk on the beach and waded along the shore after our lunch of delicious clams. I was feeling sad that I would soon be taking the train back north to the city and home. Gram noticed that I was unhappy. She gave me a hug and told me not to worry. "You'll be back soon—now that you have sand in your shoes."

乎全白色。太姥姥在盘子上放了一个蚌，教我怎样把蚌口的皮剥掉。剥好了，她就递给我吃。

"祝你好胃口，"吉姆说，"享受美味吧！"

蚌好吃极了。再配上鲜面包和冰柠檬水，这简直是我吃过最美味的大餐了。

告别

吃完美味的蚌肉午餐之后，太姥姥、吉姆和我在海滩散步了很长时间，沿着海岸深一脚浅一脚地走。想到就要坐火车北上回到城市，回到家里，我就觉得伤心。太姥姥看出我不太开心，她拥抱了我，告诉我不必不开心。"你身上有了大海的气息，你很快就会再回来的。"

---

delicious *adj.* 美味的   lemonade *n.* 柠檬水

Sea gulls kept flying to a pair of huge rocks nearby. Jim helped me climb to the top so I could see what the birds liked so much. On top, I found a small pool of water. I felt very tall standing on the rock. I could see far out into the ocean and up and down the beach. This was a perfect place for sea gulls to *perch*. This was a perfect place for me to say my goodbyes.

海鸥不断地飞到附近的两块巨石上来。吉姆帮我爬到巨石上面，看看是什么吸引了那些海鸥。在岩石高处，我看到了一小汪水。站在巨石上，我觉得自己很高大。辽阔的大海，高高低低的海滩，尽收眼底。这确实是海鸥栖息的理想去处。这也是我进行告别的最佳地点。

---

perch *v.* 栖息

8

Samson: A Horse Story

The Letter

•June 4

I can't believe I'm in the back seat of the car instead of at the pool. Who is Aunt Rita anyway? Why would she leave Dad a *stinky* old farm? It's sad that she died, but this woman, who I had never heard of until today, has ruined my summer.

I wish the letter had gotten lost in the mail. Then Dad would never have known that his aunt left him a farm in Kentucky. Mom and Dad

---

马匹萨姆森的故事

来信

• 6月4日

我真不敢相信我没在游泳池里，却在汽车后座上。到底谁是丽塔阿姨？她为什么要给爸爸留下一个又臭又旧的农场呢？她的过世是很令人伤心，但她也不该毁掉我的暑假——我今天才第一次听说这个人。

我真希望那封信当时就邮丢了。那样爸爸就永远不会知道他的阿姨在

---

stinky *adj.* 发臭的

are teachers. What do they know about being farmers?

• June 5

I was slipping down the pool slide when I smelled something horrible. Then I saw it. The pool was filled with cow *manure*! I tried to stop, but I couldn't, and just as my toes were about to slip into the pool, I woke up. Whew, it was just a dream, but then the smell hit me hard. I sprang up in my seat. We were turning into the farm's *driveway*. I plugged my nose and tried not to breathe.

A man and a boy dressed in overalls waved to us from the front porch. The boy looked a few years older than me. Dad said that Mr. Winn and his 15-year-old son, Henry, would be showing us around the farm. All I wanted to do was go to bed. I grabbed my *suitcase* and walked inside.

肯塔基给他留了个农场。爸爸妈妈都是教师，他们哪知道怎么做农活呢？

• 6月5日

我正从泳池的滑坡进到水里时，突然闻到了很难闻的味道。然后，我就看见整个泳池都是牛粪！我想停住脚步，却停不下来，就在我的脚趾要滑进水里时，我一下子醒了。喔，好在只是个梦，但是那股臭味却让我记忆犹新。我从后座上弹了起来。我们已经开进了农场的车道。我堵住了鼻孔，还尽力屏住呼吸。

有一个男人和一个孩子在前门向我们挥手，他们两人都穿着套头毛衣。那个小男孩看着比我大几岁。爸爸说，韦恩先生和他15岁的儿子会领我们在农场四处看看。但我却只是想睡上一觉。我抓起了手提箱，走了进去。

---

manure *n.* 粪便   driveway *n.* 车道

suitcase *n.* 手提箱

Mom said I could have first pick of the bedrooms, so I dragged my suitcase up the stairs. There were three bedrooms. I chose the one that faced away from the farm. Maybe, I thought, hat would help me forget where I was.

• June 7

I can't believe how slow time passes around here. I've never been so bored. I miss the pool. I miss my friends. I'd rather be at school than here on this stinky old farm. I'm *avoiding* Dad. He's mad at me because I'm not helping out. It's his farm; let him do the work!

• June 9

Dad yelled at me at dinner. He said I'd best stop feeling sorry for myself and start *pitching in*. I refused to look at him because I didn't

---

妈妈说我可以先选卧室，我就拖着行李箱上了楼梯。共有三间卧室。我选了一间看不见农场的。我想，也许这样我就能忘记身在农场了。

• 6月7日

真是难以相信在农场的时间过得这么慢。我从未感觉到如此无聊。我想念游泳池。我想念朋友们。我宁愿上学也不想待在这个又旧又臭的农场。我不想见爸爸，他见我不出去帮忙干活就大发脾气。这是他的农场；活都留给他干吧！

• 6月9日

晚饭时，爸爸对我大吼起来。他说我最好别在这垂头丧气的，应该和

---

avoid *v.* 躲开（人、事物）

pitch in 参与；出力

want him to see me crying. I just stared at my plate.

Dad said, starting tomorrow morning, I have to help Henry *tend to* the animals. "Tend to" the animals? Dad acts like he really is a farmer.

Meeting Samson

• June 10

Mom woke me at five this morning so I could meet Henry at six. Why do farmers wake up so early?

Henry was working in the *barn* when he saw me. He waved hello and said he had heard I wasn't too eager to help out, so I could just

---

家人一起干活。我没有抬头看他，因为我不想让他看见我的眼泪。我的眼睛只盯着自己的盘子。

爸爸说，明早开始，我就去帮亨利照料牲口。"照料"牲口？爸爸现在真像个地道的农民。

见到萨姆森

• 6月10日

妈妈早上5点就把我叫醒了，这样我才能赶在6点见到亨利。农民们为什么要起这么早呢？

我见到亨利时，他正在马厩里干活。他和我打招呼，说他听说我不想出来干活，所以我只要跟着他到处看看就好了。至少还有亨利理解我。

---

tend to 照料   barn *n.* 马厩

follow him around and watch. At least Henry understands me.

I trailed along as Henry cleaned out the chicken coop. It was *disgusting*! When he was done, Henry collected some eggs and dropped them gently into a basket. They were all different colors—not like the eggs at the *supermarket* back at home.

Then we headed to a small barn. Henry opened the top half of the door, and much to my surprise a reddish-orange horse poked its head through the door. A thick, white stripe *split* its face in two. I didn't know Aunt Rita had a horse.

Henry introduced me to Samson and asked if I liked horses. I lied and said I thought they were okay. Actually, I don't like them and can't understand why so many girls my age do. I watched as Henry opened the bottom half of the door and led Samson to a fenced

亨利清理鸡笼的时候，我就跟在他身后。真恶心！亨利清理完鸡笼，又开始捡鸡蛋，再把鸡蛋轻轻放到篮子里。鸡蛋的颜色各不相同——我家那边超市的鸡蛋可都是一个颜色的。

然后我们去了小马厩。亨利打开上半扇门，我没想到有一匹橘红色的马把头从门里伸了出来，马头正中有一条白色的宽条纹。我没听说丽塔阿姨还有一匹马。

亨利告诉了萨姆森我叫什么名，又问我喜不喜欢马。我撒谎说我觉得马挺可爱的。其实，我一点也不喜欢马，也不理解我同龄的女孩子们怎么会喜欢马。我看到亨利打开了下半扇门，将萨姆森领到了一片有栅栏的牧场。

disgusting *adj.* 恶心的　　　　　　　　supermarket *n.* 超市
split *v.* 分开

area.

He said that Samson liked to graze on grass during the morning, and that we would come back later and feed him some oats. He fetched a hose and brought it to a big metal trough, which he filled with water.

As he walked back with the hose, he *tripped* over a big, white block. He asked if I knew what it was. I didn't really care. He said it was a salt block and that horses need to lick salt blocks because they lose a lot of salt when they sweat.

Then Henry accused Samson of moving the salt block so he would trip on it. "Maybe he's mad because Rita died," he added. Then he grabbed a brush and began *stroking* the horse with it. He talked quietly to Samson as he *groomed* him. Samson didn't seem mad to me.

亨利说萨姆森早上喜欢吃草，我们等一下会回来，喂它吃些麦片粥。他把一根水管拿到了一个金属的大水槽那里，把水槽注满了水。

亨利拿着水管回来的时候，绊倒在一个白色大砖块上。他问我知不知道那是什么东西。我其实没想知道。他说这是一块盐砖，马需要舔盐砖，因为马在流汗时会流失大量盐分。

然后亨利"控诉"说，是萨姆森挪动了盐砖，他才绊倒在上面的。"也许是丽塔的去世让它变得不正常了，"亨利又说道。他接着又抓起一把刷子，轻刷起马身。他边梳理着萨姆森的毛发，边和萨姆森说话。我看萨姆森没什么不正常的。

---

trip *v.* 绊；绊倒   stroke *v.* 抚摩；轻抚
groom *v.* 洗刷（动物）

• June 21

I know why Aunt Rita named her horse Samson. *According to* her journal, she liked a boy named James Samson who worked on the farm. She liked to watch him, but she was too shy to talk to him. One day he asked her if she wanted to ride one of the horses. She didn't like horses, but she agreed because she anted to be friends with James.

She rode a reddish-orange horse named Jack. He had a white stripe down his nose, just as Samson does. Rita was *nervous* about riding, but she trusted James. She wrote all about her first ride in her journal. It seemed to change her. Riding horses couldn't bring her mom back, she wrote, but now she had something to *look forward to* each day.

• 6月21日

我知道了丽塔阿姨为什么给马起名叫萨姆森。她的日记里写着,她喜欢一个在农场工作的男孩——詹姆斯·萨姆森。她喜欢看着他做事情,但是自己太害羞,不敢和他讲话。有一天,男孩问她想不想骑马试试。尽管她不喜欢马,她还是答应试试,因为她想和詹姆斯成为朋友。

她骑上了一匹橘红色的马,名叫杰克。这匹马的鼻子下方有一条白毛,就像那匹叫萨姆森的马一样。丽塔骑马时很紧张,但她信任詹姆斯。她在日记里详细地记述了第一次骑马的情景。这次经历仿佛改变了她。她写道,骑马并不能让她的妈妈复生,但是她现在每天都有了一些盼头。

---

according to 根据   nervous *adj.* 紧张的
look forward to 期待

Mr. Winn and Henry had dinner with us tonight. After dinner I asked Henry if I could ride Samson tomorrow. He said yes!

The Ride

• June 22

When I got to the barn, I started helping Henry *right away*. I think he was surprised because I usually don't help much. I just wanted to finish the chores so we could ride.

As we headed to Samson's stall, I realized how much I had learned about taking care of farm animals. I've even gotten used to the smell. Henry asked why I had changed my mind about riding Samson. I didn't want to tell him about Aunt Rita's *journal*. He might not think I should be into her private things, so I told him I was bored instead.

今晚，韦恩先生和亨利同我们共进晚餐。饭后，我问亨利我明天可不可以骑萨姆森试试，他说当然可以！

骑马

• 6月22日

我一到马厩，立刻开始帮亨利干活。我觉得亨利一定吓到了，因为我通常都不太帮忙。我只是想快点干完活，然后就可以骑马了。

我们走向萨姆森所在隔间的时候，我突然意识到我已经懂得了很多关于照料家畜的知识。我甚至已经习惯了农场的气味。亨利问我为什么改变想法，想要骑萨姆森了。我不想对他讲丽塔阿姨日记的事，他可能会觉得我不该翻看丽塔阿姨的私人物件，所以我对他说，我只是觉得太无聊了。

---

right away 立刻   journal *n.* 日记

When Henry opened the barn, Samson looked different to me. He seemed handsome. His colors were brighter. I think he even smiled at me. Henry put Samson's *saddle* on and dragged a *stepladder* next to his side. I climbed on. Henry guided my left foot into the *stirrup* and then helped me swing my right leg up and over Samson's back.

Henry gave me a few pointers about how to ride before he led me and Samson out to the pasture. I held onto the reins and the saddle horn with all my might as we walked along.

Riding a horse was just as Aunt Rita had described it—a little scary, but also very exciting. I kept thinking: What if I fall? What if Samson starts *galloping*? What if he tries to throw me off? Yet he was so gentle. I couldn't believe I was riding a horse and liking it. I

亨利打开马厩时，我看到了一个不一样的萨姆森。它看起来很英俊，毛色也更亮，我甚至觉得它在对我笑呢。亨利给萨姆森安上马鞍，又在萨姆森身旁拉出了一条折梯。我爬了上去。亨利让我把左脚放进马镫，然后帮我抬起右腿，跨到萨姆森的背上。

亨利在放我和萨姆森到牧场之前，先给我讲了几点有关骑马的技巧。我们往外走的时候，我死死地抓住了缰绳和鞍角。

骑马的感觉就和丽塔阿姨描述的一样——有点害怕，但也非常刺激。我一直在想：要是我摔下来怎么办？要是萨姆森飞奔起来怎么办？要是萨姆森想把我从马背上抛下来怎么办？但是萨姆森十分温和。我简直不敢相

---

saddle *n.* 马鞍
stirrup *n.* 马镫

stepladder *n.* 折梯
gallop *v.* 飞奔

couldn't *believe* I was having fun!

• June 26

I spent the last few days taking riding lessons from Henry. But it rained today, so I read more of Aunt Rita's journal.

About six months after Rita started riding Jack, her dad announced that they were moving back to New York City. He was too sad living in the town where Rita's mom had died. Rita was sad too—and mad. She didn't want to leave James or Jack. After losing her mom, she couldn't believe she was losing everything else too.

That's how her journal ended.

信我在骑马，而且很喜欢骑马的感觉。我不敢相信骑马给我带来了很大的乐趣！

• 6月26日

这几天，我一直在和亨利学习骑马。但是今天下雨了，所以我又继续读起丽塔阿姨的日记来。

丽塔开始骑马大约六个月以后，她爸爸说他们要搬回纽约市去了。丽塔的妈妈在这个镇子去世，他住在这里感到伤心不能自已。丽塔也很伤心——还有点发狂。她不想离开詹姆斯，也不想离开杰克。她已经失去了妈妈，她无法相信，连剩下的一切也要失去了。

她的日记就写到这里。

---

believe *v.* 相信

I wanted to find out more about Aunt Rita. I asked Mom if the Winns could come to dinner. That's when I told them about the journal and how it ended. Mr. Winn explained that Rita never forgot Jack, and as soon as she was able she moved back to the country and bought herself another horse. And in her eighties, she was still quite the rider.

I wanted to know why she left the farm to Dad. Mr. Winn smiled and said that Aunt Rita knew about me, and she knew I was the only young girl in the family tree. She wanted a young girl to *look after* Samson.

Then Dad said we needed to *discuss* what would happen to the farm when it was time to go back home.

我想知道更多关于丽塔阿姨的事，于是问妈妈韦恩父子俩会不会来吃晚餐。他们来的时候，我就对他们讲了日记的事，还有日记的结尾。韦恩先生说，丽塔从未忘记杰克。她后来等到条件一允许，就回到农村，自己又买了一匹马。丽塔阿姨直到八十几岁仍然是很棒的骑手。

我想知道她为什么把农场留给了我爸爸。韦恩先生笑着说，丽塔阿姨知道我的存在，也知道我是家族里唯一的小女孩。她希望有一个小女孩来照顾萨姆森。

然后爸爸说，我们要讨论一下回家以后农场怎么办。

---

look after　照顾

discuss　*v.* 讨论

Leaving Samson

• June 27

Dad is actually *considering* selling the farm. And he says if he does sell it, he'll sell everything along with it, including Samson. He says he's just not ready to own a farm because it's too much work.

I told him that I wouldn't let him do it! After all, Samson is mine. Aunt Rita wanted me to have him. I love him. There is no way that I'll let Dad sell him.

• July 1

Mr. Winn came by to see Dad and Mom last night. He offered to take care of the farm during the school year, while we're away. Dad

---

告别萨姆森

• 6月27日

其实爸爸在考虑卖掉农场。他说，如果卖掉农场的话，就会把农场的一切都卖掉，包括萨姆森。他说自己没有准备好经营农场，农活也太繁重了，干不过来。

我告诉他，我不同意！毕竟，萨姆森属于我了。丽塔阿姨希望我照顾萨姆森。我爱萨姆森。我绝不能让爸爸把萨姆森卖掉。

• 7月1日

昨晚，韦恩先生路过，来看爸爸妈妈。他提议说，我们在学年期间不

---

consider *v.* 考虑

said he'd think about it. I hate it when he says that!

• July 7

It's a done deal! Dad *agreed* to keep the farm. He hired Mr. Winn to run it for us. I've never been so happy. As soon as I heard the news I ran out to tell Samson. I think he understood.

• July 18

I can't believe I have to go home. Mom and Dad need to get their classrooms ready for the new school year. I'm sure going to miss Mr. Winn, Henry, and everything about Aunt Rita's house. But most of all, I'll miss Samson. I can't wait to get back to him and that old

---

在农场时，他可以代为照顾。爸爸说他要考虑一下。我真讨厌听他说还要考虑！

• 7月7日

就这么说定了！爸爸同意留着农场，并雇佣韦恩先生来经营农场。我感觉高兴极了。一听说这个消息，我就跑出去告诉萨姆森，我相信它能听懂。

• 7月18日

真不敢相信我得回家了。爸爸妈妈要去布置教室，为新学年做好准备。我肯定会想念韦恩先生、亨利，和丽塔阿姨家里所有东西的。但是我最想念的，还是萨姆森。我迫不及待地想回去骑马，回到那个旧农场去，

---

agree *v.* 同意

farm, even if it is a little stinky.

Explore More About Horses

Horses are mammals. They *belong to* the Equus family—the same family as *zebras*, mules, and donkeys.

Horse Talk

foal a baby horse

yearling a horse between one and two years old

colt a male horse under three years old

filly a *female* horse under three years old

stallion an adult male horse

mare an adult female horse

pony a full-grown small horse

就算有点臭味又算什么呢。

更多关于马的知识

马是哺乳动物，属于"马属"——与斑马、骡子和驴属同一科。

有关"马"的表达

foal	马驹
yearling	1-2岁的马
colt	3岁以内的雄性小马
filly	3岁以内的雌性小马
stallion	成年公马
mare	成年母马
pony	长成的矮种马

---

belong to 属于   zebra *n.* 斑马

female *adj.* 雌性的

A mare carries her baby for 11 months. Most mares give birth in the spring to one baby, but twins are not *uncommon*. It takes three to four years for a horse to fully *mature*.

Horses *generally* live to be between 20 and 25 years old, although they can live for up to 30 years. The oldest recorded horse was Old Billy, an English barge horse, who lived to be 62 years old.

母马通常怀胎11个月。大多数母马会在春季产一匹小马，但是双胞胎马也很常见。一匹马要完全长成，需要3至4年的时间。

马的平均寿命约为20至25岁，有些马的寿命可能长达30岁。史上最长寿的马为英国的驳马"老比利"，寿命达62岁。

---

uncommon *adj.* 不常见的   mature *v.* 发育成熟
generally *adv.* 一般地

9

Saved by the stars

Lost

"Go left!" Trevon shouted.

"No, go right!" Leo yelled.

Miguel Ventura pedaled hard, glancing down at a map drawn on the palm of his hand. He'd been *sweating*, and as the sun set, Miguel could barely make out the lines and street names. "We'd better *pull over*."

星星的救赎

迷路

"往左边走!"特雷弗喊到。

"不对,往右边走!"利奥叫嚷着。

米格尔·范杜拉一边瞟着画在他手掌上的地图,一边艰难地蹬着自行车。他已经大汗淋漓,而且因为太阳已经下山了,米格尔几乎无法辨认出线路和街道的名字。"我们最好靠边停下。"

---

sweat *v.* 出汗　　　　　　　　　　pull over 靠路边停车

The three boys hopped their bikes up a curb and skidded into a driveway.

"I think this line is San Martin Avenue." Miguel pointed to a *crease* on his palm.

"No, dude, that's your lifeline," said Leo. "And it's looking pretty short unless you find the baseball field."

"The Black Cobras finally *challenged* us to a game," said Trevon as he smacked his ball into his glove, "and thanks to you, they'll think we *chickened out*."

"I thought it ... I mean, it should be right here."

"You got us lost," Leo said.

三个男孩骑着自行车蹦上了马路边，把车停在了一个私家车道上。

"我认为这条是圣马丁大街。"米格尔指着他手掌上的一条皱纹说道。

"不，老兄，那是你的生命线。"利奥说道："而且你如果找不到棒球场，它看起来就会非常短。"

"黑眼镜蛇队终于邀请我们赛一场比试高低了。"特雷弗一边说一边啪地一声把棒球扔进了他的手套里。"托你的福，他们会以为我们临阵退缩的。"

"我认为它……我是说，它应该就在这里。"

"你让我们迷路了。"利奥说道。

---

crease *n.* 皱纹   challenge *v.* 挑战
chicken out 临阵退缩

Miguel *swallowed* and glanced down at his sweaty hand. The *moisture* had erased almost all the ink-drawn lines. The sky grew dim and Miguel glanced up, scanning for stars. Sailors from long ago used them to *navigate*. But the heavens, a mucky gray, had not darkened enough to show even the first star. Oh, how he longed to make a wish.

"Let's go." Miguel pumped his pedals down another street, but what he thought was a shortcut quickly led to a dead end. The boys swerved down a side alley. Something creaked behind them. Miguel's heart raced. Trevon and Leo *breathed* hard as they sped away.

米格尔咽了一口唾沫，又低头扫了一眼他那汗津津的手。汗的潮湿几乎抹掉了所有的墨水画成的线条。天色渐暗，米格尔抬头望去，扫视天空寻找着星星。很久以来，水手们就用星星来导航。但天空却是污染的灰蒙蒙一片，天还没有完全黑下来，甚至连启明星都还看不到。哦，他是多么渴望能许个愿啊！

"我们走吧。"米格尔蹬着自行车沿着另外一条路骑了下去，但他本以为是条捷径的路却很快让他们骑进了死胡同。男孩们猛地转向进了一个小胡同。在他们身后有什么东西在吱吱作响。米格尔的心跳加速。特雷弗和利奥的呼吸变得沉重，他们一起飞快地离开了那儿。

---

swallow *v.* 吞
navigate *v.* 导航

moisture *v.* 潮湿
breath *v.* 呼吸

Bang! Crash! Trashcans fell. Rats skittered down the gutter.

The boys slid out to a stop under a darkened *streetlamp*, crashing into one another like dominoes.

"Where's the field?" Trevon yelled, unwrapping himself from Leo, who looked just as angry as Trevon.

Miguel stood up, sweat poured from under his bike *helmet*. "It should be right here."

"You need a GPS, man," Leo said.

The sun had completely *vanished* along with Miguel's hope of finding the field. The pressure jumbled Miguel's brain. Street names.

砰！一声巨响！垃圾桶被撞翻了，老鼠们飞快地跑进路边的水沟。

男孩们侧滑着停在了一个昏暗的路灯下，像多米诺骨牌一样撞到了一起。

"棒球场在哪儿啊？"特雷弗一边叫嚷着，一边从利奥的纠缠中把自己解脱出来，而利奥看起来也和特雷弗一样得愤怒。

米格尔站了起来，汗水从他的自行车头盔里倾泻而下。"球场就应该在这儿啊。"

"兄弟，你需要个全球定位系统了。"利奥说道。

米格尔想要找到球场的希望伴随着太阳一起彻底地消失了。压力让米

---

streetlamp *n.* 路灯　　　　　　　　　　　　　　helmet *n.* 头盔
vanish *v.* 消失

Intersections. Buildings. They all ran together like one big mass of information. The map was useless. The game was totally lost. And so were they.

"Come on, Leo," Trevon said. "We're out of here."

Horsing Around

"Great sense of *direction*," Leo said the next day at school. Both he and Trevon blamed Migueleld for not finding the field. To make things worse, Miguel felt one of the boys from the Black Cobras left a rubber chicken in Trevon's backpack. Miguel felt *horrible* for letting his friends down, but he didn't know what to do to make it up to them.

格尔的大脑乱成一锅粥。街道的名字，十字路口，建筑物，这一大堆杂乱的信息拥挤在一起。那地图根本就没用。比赛彻底地输掉了。而他们也一样彻底地迷路了。

"来吧，利奥。"特雷弗说："让我们离开这儿。"

摩登骑士精神

"方向感真好。"第二天利奥在学校说着反话。他和特雷弗把没有找到球场归咎于米格尔。更糟糕的是，黑眼镜蛇队的一个男孩儿还在特雷弗的背包里放了一只橡胶小鸡来讽刺他。让他的朋友们失望使米格尔感觉糟透了，但他也不知道该做些什么去补偿他们。

---

direction *n.* 方向   horrible *adj.* 糟糕的

After school, Miguel found himself all alone, so he *sulked* up to the loft in the back of his family's sandwich shop. It was here that he had found his great-grandpa Gallardo's magic books. These books made the best medicine. By some magic, he could escape into one of the stories, which always helped him forget his problems.

A new book, *Black Beauty*, lay atop the chest. Miguel studied the small golden star inlaid on the book's cover. He'd read the story about the life and *treatment* of this amazing horse to his sister Teresa last year. Teresa loved horses. On page 107, Miguel began to read, "Wake up, Beauty! You will have to run as fast as you can!" This must have been the part where Black Beauty had to race all night to

---

放学的时候，米格尔发现自己孤身一人，于是他闷闷不乐地到他家三明治店身后的阁楼去了。就是在那儿他发现了他曾祖父盖拉多的有魔力的书。这些书是最好的药剂。通过一些魔法，他能够逃进到其中的一个故事里去，这通常能帮助他忘记所面临的难题。

一本新书，《黑骏马》，就躺在箱子顶上。米格尔研究着嵌入书封面的小金星。去年他就给他的妹妹特丽莎读过关于这匹神奇的马的一生以及对待它的态度。特丽莎很喜欢马。在第107页，米格尔开始读着，"醒过来，黑骏马！你必须能有多快就跑多快！"这一句是讲黑骏马不得不全速

---

sulk *v.* 闷闷不乐　　　　　　　　　　treatment *n.* 对待

the doctor. The horse didn't get lost Miguel thought to himself.

The words danced around on the page.

"Happening had Before my the I was saddle knew back. what he the on..."

Pressure spread across my ribs. Then all went dark. I awoke to the smell of hay in a stable and found myself standing in a stall... on four legs! My long black tail swished behind me. Metal horseshoes were tacked to each one of my hooves— I have hooves! A metal bar ran across my teeth. Every time I bit down, it felt cold and hard, and almost made me gag. Before I could think about being a horse, two men came up from behind me.

快跑一整夜去看医生的那一段。那马可没迷路，米格尔暗自想着。

纸面上的字开始翩翩起舞。

"在我之前发生了……我回来只知道马鞍……他在……"

压力传遍了我的肋骨。接着一切都变得漆黑一片。我醒来闻到了马厩里干草的气息，发现自己站在畜栏里……四脚着地！我的长长的黑色尾巴在身后嗖嗖地挥摆着。我的每一只蹄子上都钉上金属马掌——我居然有蹄子！一根金属棒横穿过我上下牙齿之间。每当我咬牙的时候，都感觉冷冰冰，硬邦邦的，而且几乎让我作呕。在我还没来得及考虑如何作一匹马的时候，两个人从我身后走过来。

---

pressure *n.* 压力

A younger man in riding gear hopped on my back.

"Ride as fast as you can, John," said a guy wearing a black tuxedo. "Our *mistress*'s life *depends upon* it."

He gave John a note. "Give this to Dr. White and be sure to rest the horse. Return as soon as you can!"

With that, John dug his *heels* into my sides and off I ran, down the path and into the hills. "Do your best. We must save our mistress's life!"

As Black Beauty, it was up to me to save the life of my owner's wife! A rush of *adrenaline* surged through me. But as I ran ahead, my legs almost froze. What if I couldn't make it like Black Beauty

---

一个年轻人穿着骑马装跳到我的背上。

"约翰，尽你所能有多快骑多快。"一个身穿晚礼服的家伙说："我们女主人的命就依赖于它了。"

他递给约翰一张纸条。"把它交给怀特医生，并一定要让马休息一下。然后尽快返回。"

带上纸条，约翰用他的脚后跟戳着我的肋部，于是我撒开四蹄奔跑起来，沿着小路进入山中。"要全力以赴啊。我们一定要挽救女主人的生命。"

作为黑骏马，必须由我来挽救主人太太的生命！一股肾上腺素如波涛般汹涌奔流传遍我全身。但随着我向前跑，我的腿几乎动弹不得。如果我

---

mistress *n.* 女主人　　　　　　　　depend upon 依赖

heel *n.* 脚后跟　　　　　　　　　　adrenaline *n.* 肾上腺素

had in the *original* story? It would be my fault if the mistress died. The weight of that idea was heavier than the rider on my back, but I galloped as hard as I could, knowing the owner had never let Beauty down.

The sun faded as we followed trails that wound through thick pine forest. But I barely noticed my surroundings as John *skillfully* steered me with the reins.

My eyelids *drooped*. My legs ached. We had been riding all night, and I wasn't sure I could go any farther. Luckily for me, it wasn't long before we reached Dr. White's house. John pounded at the door, but the doctor did not come out. I whinnied as loud as I could, but there was no Dr. White to be found.

没办法像原著中黑骏马那样成功办到该怎么办？如果女主人死去那就是我的过错。那想法的沉重感远比在我背上的骑手来得重，但我还是尽可能地奋力疾驰，因为我知道主人从来没有让黑骏马失望过。

当我们寻着踪迹曲曲折折穿过浓密松树林的时候，太阳消失了。但是由于约翰熟练地用缰绳驾驭着我，让我几乎注意不到周围的事物。

我的眼皮开始下垂。我的腿疼痛难忍。我们已经骑了一整夜了，我不确定我还能再走多远。所幸的是，不久以后我们便到达了怀特医生的家。约翰重重地敲了敲门，但医生没有出来。我尽自己最大的声音叫着，却没有发现怀特医生的踪影。

---

original *adj.* 原著的　　　　　　　　　　　skillfully *adv.* 巧妙地
droop *v.* 下垂

Finally, after much *hollering* and banging, a man in his *nightshirt* threw open the window. John explained our situation.

"My horse is sick," said the doctor, *adjusting* his glasses. "I must ride back on yours."

My heart dropped. I looked at John. He *grimaced*, knowing full well how exhausted I was.

"My horse needs rest," John said, placing a hand on my shoulder. "I don't know whether Black Beauty will make it."

"It's the only way to save the mistress," the doctor said as he picked up his black case.

John was like Beauty's owner in that he would never have allowed the doctor to ride me back without rest if not for such dire

---

最终，在一阵大呼小叫和乒乓作响的敲门声之后，一个穿着睡衣的男人猛地打开了窗户，约翰向他解释了一下我们的处境。

"我的马病了。"医生一边调整了一下他的眼镜，一边说道："我必须骑你的马回去。"

我的心一下子沉了下去。我看着约翰，他皱着眉头，完全清楚地知道我已经是多么得筋疲力尽了。

"我的马需要休息。"约翰把手放在我的肩膀上说："我不知道黑骏马还能不能行。"

"这是救女主人的唯一办法。"医生一边说着一边拿起了他的黑色手提箱。

约翰和黑骏马的主人一样，要不是因为如此严峻的形势，他是绝对不

---

holler *v.* 大声叫喊　　　　　　　　nightshirt *n.* 睡衣
adjust *v.* 调整　　　　　　　　　　grimace *v.* （因痛苦）脸部扭曲

circumstances.

After a long drink, my *muscles* tightened as the old man climbed upon me. He didn't feel as sure of himself on my back as John had. I whinnied and neighed—*swished* my head and tail. Then I stomped my feet.

"Settle down, Beauty," John said, "this is life or death. Your mistress needs you now more than ever."

A Slippery Setback

"Hee-yah!" The doctor snapped the reins together as I *traversed* a field. He tapped my sides with his heels, and I ran forward through the trails and into a meadow. I passed into the pine forest and the doctor dug his heels into my sides further. As I galloped, a pain

---

会让我不休息就允许医生骑着我的。

痛快地喝了一大口水后，当那老人爬到我身上，我的肌肉又紧绷了起来。他骑在我的背上感觉并不像约翰一般自信。我不停摆动着头和尾巴，嗖嗖地嘶鸣着然后我开始跺起脚来。

"平静下来，黑骏马。"约翰说道："这是生死攸关的时刻。你的女主人现在比以往任何时候都更需要你。"

灾难性的挫折

"驾！"当我穿过一片旷野时，医生把缰绳紧紧地抓在一起。他用脚跟轻叩着我的肋部，我向前跑着。穿过崎岖的小路跑进一片大草地。然后

---

circumstance *n.* 形势；情形

swish *v.* 快速移动

muscle *n.* 肌肉

traverse *v.* 穿过

shot up my rear leg, as if the *tendons* were about to snap like rubber bands. My heart thumped, and I breathed out hard through my nostrils. The chill transformed my breath into steam, and I *shuddered*.

"This way!" the doctor shouted, pulling me to the right.

I ran ahead, every step sending a burst of pain throughout my body. Even this slight man *equaled* the weight of fifty sandbags.

We passed what felt like a thousand trees. A weird, white froth *foamed* from my mouth. I felt the doctor's hands loosen on my He must have been getting tired, too. Once out of the forest, we approached a ridge. A fierce wind howled against my face as if I

进入到松树林，医生用脚跟在我的肋部戳得更深了。随着我不断地疾驰，后腿的疼痛也不断加剧，肌腱就好像是橡皮筋就要突然拉断一样。我的心脏砰砰直跳，通过鼻孔沉重地呼着气。寒风将我的呼吸凝结成水蒸气状，我浑身战栗着。

"走这边！"医生喊道，牵引着我转向右边。

我向前跑着，每跑一步全身都会发出一阵剧痛。即使是如此瘦小的男人也让我感觉如同是五十个沙袋那样沉重。

我们感觉好似经过了一千棵树。我的嘴里吐出来奇怪的白色的泡沫。感觉到医生抓着我的缰绳的双手也渐渐松了下来，他也一定变得很疲惫

tendon *n.* 腱；肌腱　　　　　　　　　　shudder *v.* 战栗

equal *v.* 等同　　　　　　　　　　　　　foam *v.* 吐白沫

were moving forward against a wall. As we neared a steeply sloping, rocky trail, the doctor stopped me. "Steady," he whispered as he gently *nudged* me into the *descent*.

I tried to place my hooves down solidly, but each step was a chore. My legs tingled with numbness. Left. Right. Left... My right hind leg slipped on a piece of shale, and down I went.

My fall stretched out for what felt like minutes. *Gravity* tore the doctor to the ground. My body seemed to drop, inch by inch, until my side slammed against rocks at the hill's bottom.

I lay there, my neck and shoulders wet with sweat, *wrenching* in

---

了。一出树林，我们就来到一处山脊。狂风呼啸着吹到我的脸上，那感觉就好像撞到了一面墙上一样。当我们接近了一处陡峭的碎石斜坡时，医生让我停了下来。"稳住。"他一边轻轻地推着我向斜坡下面走一边低声说道。

我试图把蹄子都踩得稳当些，但每一步都很艰难。我的腿伴随着麻木开始刺痛起来。左，右，左……我的右后腿在一片页岩上滑了一下，接着我便摔了下去。

我一直往下跌着，感觉好像持续了几分钟一样。地心引力将医生重重地撞倒在地。我的身体似乎在一点一点地往下掉，直到我的肋部重重地撞到山脚下的岩石上。

---

nudge *v.* 轻推
gravity *n.* 重力

descent *n.* 下坡
wrench *v.* 使痛苦

pain. Somewhere behind me I heard the doctor moan. All I could think about was the mistress and how she would not make it. And it would be my fault. Soon cold blackness overtook my body, but the white-hot pain *remained*.

Sightless

Crickets chirped in my ears, and strangely enough I heard each of them sing in a different key, like a chorus. My eyelids *fluttered*, welcoming in the darkness of night. For the first time I realized that as a horse my night *vision* had improved.

I turned my head at movement in the trees; but the pain stopped me. Every square inch of my body hurt. Gently pushing from my

---

　　我躺在那儿，脖子和肩膀都大汗淋漓，疼痛难忍。我听到身后传来了医生的呻吟声。我脑海中唯一想到的就是女主人还有她可能撑不过去了的念头。而这都将是我的错。很快寒冷的黑暗便笼罩了我的身体，却只留下了白热灼烫的痛楚。

　　眼不见物

　　蟋蟀在我耳边鸣叫着，说来也奇怪，我听到它们每一只都在唱着不同的音调，就像一支合唱队。我的眼皮震颤着，迎接夜晚黑暗的到来。我第一次意识到，作为一匹马我的夜视能力提高了。

　　我回头望向树林的过程中，疼痛却阻止了我的动作。我身体的每一寸

---

remain *v.* 留下　　　　　　　　　　　　　　　flutter *v.* 震颤
vision *n.* 视力

side, I sat *upright* and stretched my neck. I flexed my legs. The muscles were stiff like drying cement, but they moved and were not broken.

"Beauty?" a hoarse voice muttered from behind me.

The doctor! He was alive! His voice shook my *jumbled* thoughts back to reality.

I *scrambled* to my feet, wobbly at first, but stable. After I gained my balance, I searched the trees for the doctor. He lay spread across a bed of pine *needles*, his hands still clutching the black bag. I nudged him with my muzzle. He didn't move. I licked him on the face and he stirred.

都很痛。缓缓地用肋部向上拱，直立地坐了起来，伸展着我的脖子。伸缩了一下我的腿。肌肉僵硬得像干燥的水泥一样，但腿还能动并没有坏掉。

"黑骏马？"我身后低声传来了一个嘶哑的声音。

医生！他还活着！他的声音把我从混乱的思绪中又摇回到现实中来。

我匆忙站了起来，一开始摇摇晃晃地，后来还是站稳了。在我保持平衡以后，便开始在树林里寻找医生。他躺在遍布着一层松针的那块地上，手里仍然紧紧抓着那黑色的医药包。我用嘴轻轻地推了推他。他一动也不动。我用舌头舔他的脸，他苏醒了过来。

---

upright *adj.* 直立的
scramble *v.* （迅速而吃力地）爬

jumbled *adj.* 混乱的
needle *n.* 针

"Ah, you are a beauty." The doctor arose slowly and came to a stance. He squinted, then dropped to the ground, feeling around for something. "I lost my glasses in the fall; I can't see a thing!"

His glasses! I *swiveled* my head around and tried to paw the ground, but it was useless without fingers.

"I got them!" the doctor shouted. But before he could slip his glasses on, his face dropped. And I knew exactly why. The *lenses* had fallen out in the crash.

He glanced around, then walked over and stroked my neck. "It's up to you now, Beauty. Get us home. Take us to the mistress." Doctor White placed his feet in the stirrups and climbed onto my back.

"啊，你真是匹骏马啊。"医生慢慢地起身并站了起来。他眯起眼睛，然后趴在地上，四处摸索着在找什么东西。"在跌倒的时候我把眼镜弄丢了，我什么都看不到了！"

他的眼镜！我四处转动着头，并试图在地上翻找着，但没有手指头根本一点儿用都没有。

"找到了！"医生喊道。他还没来得及戴上眼镜，脸色就沉了下来。而我知道那到底是为什么。在碰撞中镜片已经脱落了。

他环顾四周，接着走过来抚摸着我的脖子。"现在全靠你了，黑骏马。让我们一起回家。带我到女主人身边去。"怀特医生把脚放在马镫里，然后爬到我的背上。

---

swivel *v.* （使）（头或眼睛）转动　　　　　lense *n.* 镜片

Look to the Sky

Fear spread across me like an icy blanket. Lost. We were lost. And now I would let the doctor and my mistress down just like I had Trevon and Leo. A long neigh *reverberated* from my throat and ended as I blew a big burst of air out my nostrils. I had the urge to rear up and run away.

"Whoa, Beauty," the doctor said. "You can do this."

His words calmed me, *seeping* down into my body like medicine.

I took one step forward. Then another. The doctor squeezed my sides just enough to get me into a full gallop. The pine needles brushed against my face. Think. I told myself. Stay calm, and think! But a fork in the road brought me to an *abrupt* halt.

仰望天空

恐惧像冰毯子似的传遍全身。迷路了。我们迷路了。而这次我要让医生和我的女主人失望了，就像我让特雷弗和利奥失望了一样。一阵长长的嘶鸣在我喉间回荡着，最后从鼻孔喷出了一大股气。我有一种冲动，要抬起前腿，后腿直立，然后逃走。

"嗨，黑骏马。"医生说道："你能行的。"

他的话语像药物一样渗入到我的身体里，使我平静了下来。

我向前迈了一步。接着又迈了一步。医生用腿挤压着我的肋部，力量刚好足够让我全速飞驰。松针擦着我的脸庞而过。思考！我告诉自己。保持镇定，思考！但是一个岔路口让我猛然停了下来。

---

reverberate *v.* 回响   seep *v.* 渗出

abrupt *adj.* 突然的

Which way, doctor? I tried to shout, but all that came out were grunts. I swung my head *back and forth*, but both paths looked the same. I had no idea where to go; I couldn't remember the way John and I came. I pawed the ground with my *hooves*.

"Use your senses, Beauty," Dr. White said. "You know the way home."

I felt totally *senseless*. My body went limp. I hung my head, and that's when I remembered the golden star that I'd found with the book.

Then I caught sight of a glittering *reflection* in a nearby stream. The water rippled and twinkled, ever so slightly, as it refl ected the

---

走哪条路，医生？我试图喊叫，但所发出来的都是咕噜声，我来回地摇摆着头，但两条路看起来一模一样。不知道该走哪条，我记不起约翰和我来时的路了。我用蹄子不断地扒着地。

"跟随你的感觉，黑骏马。"怀特医生说："你知道回家的路。"

我完全没有感觉。我的身体变得软弱无力。我低下头，就在那时我记起了在书上发现的那颗金色的星星。

然后我突然看到附近小溪里闪闪发亮的倒影。非常轻微地反射着天上的星星，水面泛起的涟漪闪烁着光芒。

---

back and forth 前前后后
senseless *adj.* 失去知觉的

hoof *n.* 蹄子
reflection *n.* 倒影

stars above.

Ideas in my brain *ignited* like sparks in dry brush. The stream ended in a lake at the manor. Of course! I needed to follow the water.

"We're going home!" I yelled, which came out in long, happy *neighs*. I shook my head and leapt around in circles.

"Whoa, Beauty!" the doctor yelled, laughing and clinging to the reins.

I stood in front of the fork in the road and I turned to the right. With the *sparkling* water shining proudly next to me, off I ran. Through the darkness. Into the hills. To the manor. To my mistress.

"Hee-yah!" the doctor yelled.

我脑中的想法如同干柴堆里的火花一般迸发出来。这小溪一直流到庄园的一个湖中。当然了！我只需要随着溪水走。

"我们要回家了！"我叫喊着，发出了一声长长的，喜悦的嘶鸣。我摇着头，兜着圈子地跳来蹦去。

"吁，黑骏马！"医生放声大笑，紧握住缰绳高声叫喊着。

我站在岔路口前，转向了右边那条路。伴随着我身旁闪闪发亮的溪水骄傲地照耀着，我飞驰而去。穿过黑暗。深入山林、跑向庄园。跑向我的女主人。

"驾！"医生叫喊着。

---

ignite *v.* 点燃   neigh *n.* 嘶鸣
sparkling *adj.* 闪闪发光的

And with that, I found myself back in the loft.

My heart still racing, I stood up and leapt in circles again. "Neeeeiighhh!" I yelled, climbing down the stairs and into the shop.

There, I found Trevon and Leo staring at me.

"What are you so happy about?" Leo asked.

"Oh, nothing," Miguel said. "Why are you guys here?"

"The Black Cobras gave us another chance," Trevon said.

"Six-thirty tonight," Leo said. "And we got the map, see?" He *fumbled* through his backpack and pulled out a yellow sheet of paper.

接着我就发现自己又回到了阁楼里。

我的心仍然在狂跳不止，我站起来又开始兜着圈子跳来蹦去。"咴儿，咴……"我像马儿一样嘶鸣着，爬下楼梯来到店里。

在那儿，我发现特雷弗和利奥正盯着我看呢。

"什么事儿让你这么高兴啊？"利奥问道。

"哦，没什么。"米格尔说："你们两个家伙怎么在这儿？"

"黑眼镜蛇队又给了我们一次机会。"特雷弗说。

"今晚六点半。"利奥说道："而且我们还有地图，看到了吗？"他在背包中摸索着，抽出一张黄色的纸。

---

fumble *v.* 摸索

"That's not a map, that's your math homework," Miguel said, laughing.

"What?" They searched the pack.

"I must have *turned in* the map instead of my homework!" Leo stomped his foot.

Miguel laughed again.

"What are you laughing at?" Trevon asked.

"Nothing."

"We're going to miss the game, again!" Leo said.

"No, don't worry, guys." Miguel *grabbed* his glove and walked toward the door. "You've got me!"

"那不是地图，是你的数学作业。"米格尔大笑着说。

"什么？"他们开始在包里搜索着。

"我一定是把我的作业当成地图装进包里了！"利奥跺了跺脚。

米格尔又大笑起来。

"你笑什么呢？"特雷弗问道。

"没什么。"

"我们要错过比赛了，再次错过！"利奥说。

"不，别担心，伙计们。"米格尔抓起手套，朝门口走去。"你们还有我呢！"

---

turn in 上交   grab *v.* 抓

10

Talking to Each Other

Even though Chris and Amanda spent a lot of time together, they never talked. Amanda didn't mind this much. In her opinion, people talked too much. That went for the girls at school, *commercials* on television, and even Mom sometimes, though that wasn't a nice thing to think. She *suspected* that Chris thought people talked too much, too, which was why they let the silence lie when they were alone together.

"Amanda! Get your shoes on. We need to go shopping," Mom yelled from the back door.

"Haaw..." Amanda groaned. She was lying in the grass, staring straight up at the *treetops* and imagining she was floating on her back in her very

---

相互沟通

虽然克里斯和阿曼达在一起度过了很多时光，但是他们从不交谈。阿曼达并不是介意这事儿。在她看来，人们说得太多了。所说的适用于学校里的女孩们，电视里的商业广告，甚至有时觉得妈妈也是这样，虽然那感觉并不是一种美好的事情。她猜想克里斯也认为人们说得太多了，这也正是为什么他们两人单独在一起时总是可以保持沉默。

"阿曼达，穿上鞋，我们要去买东西了。"妈妈从后门喊着。

"呃……"阿曼达呻吟着。她正躺在草地上，眼睛直勾勾地凝望着树顶，想象着她正仰面漂浮在她自己的游泳池里。克里斯坐在她旁边的草坪躺椅上，用他那台有着兔子耳朵般天线，用旋钮换频道的小黑白电视看着

---

commercial *n.* 商业广告　　　　　　　　　　　　　　suspect *v.* 猜想
treetop *n.* 树顶

own swimming pool. Chris sat in a lawn chair near her, watching the football game on the little black and white TV with the rabbit ears and the twist-dial channel changer. Kansas City was losing, but coming back strong, and Amanda didn't want to leave with ten minutes still on the clock.

"You hear me?" Mom shouted again, her voice coming through the windows along with the *jingle* of her keys.

"I hate shopping," Amanda said.

"You'll hate starting school in worn-out clothes even more," Mom chimed back.

"I like my clothes. I'm just going to wear out the new ones anyway," Amanda said.

Amanda felt a nudge on her leg. Chris had tapped her with his *sneaker*. He nodded toward the house, letting her know that she should stop *arguing* and go with Mom. Amanda sighed, got up, and headed inside.

"I'll let you know," Chris said, meaning the score of the game.

橄榄球赛。堪萨斯队处于劣势，但是正在强势扭转局面，阿曼达可不想在离终场还剩10分钟的时候离开。

"你听见了吗？"妈妈又喊了一次，她的声音伴着她钥匙发出的叮当声从窗户传来。

"我讨厌去购物。"阿曼达说。

"你还会更加讨厌开学穿旧衣服呢。"妈妈接着我的话茬反驳道。

"我喜欢我的衣服。反正我也会把新衣服穿旧的。"阿曼达说。

阿曼达感觉她的腿被轻轻推了一下。克里斯用他的运动鞋轻轻地碰了她一下。他朝着屋子点了点头，让她知道应该停止和妈妈犟嘴并和她一起去。阿曼达叹了一口气，站起身来，进屋去了。

"我会让你知道的。"克里斯说，意思是球赛的比分。当克里斯开口

---

jingle *n.* 叮当声   sneaker *n.* 运动鞋
argue *v.* 争辩

When he did talk, it was like that—short and *direct*, without a single *extra* word. She thought to herself that when she got home, it would be like that again. He'd say, "Twenty-one, fourteen," without *introducing* it or explaining what he meant. But she'd get it.

In the car, Mom *nervously* sipped her iced tea. Then she started talking.

"What's up, baby doll? How've you been?" she asked. Amanda wasn't sure how to answer. She saw Mom after work every day. Was there anything new she should report? "How's your summer going?" Mom pressed.

"It's going okay."

"Are you *disappointed* that you couldn't go to camp?"

"No." Amanda had gone to Lake Pines Summer Camp for the past two summers, but Mom couldn't afford to send her this year after she and Chris paid for their wedding. Amanda didn't mind

---

说话时就像那样——简短而直接，不多说一个字。阿曼达盘算着等她回家时，又将会是这个样子的。他会说："21比14"，不会对他做任何介绍和说明，但她能明白他的意思。

在车上，妈妈紧张地啜了一口冰茶，然后开始说话。

"最近怎么样？洋娃娃。过得还好吗？"她问道。阿曼达不确定该怎么回答。妈妈下班后每天她们都会见面，有什么新情况需要她报告的吗？"你暑假过得怎么样？"妈妈催促着问道。

"还不错啊。"

"没能去露营你失望吗？"

"不。"阿曼达过去的两个暑假都去了"湖岸松林"夏令营，但是今年妈妈因为和克里斯支付了婚礼的费用而负担不起送她去夏令营。阿曼达

---

direct *adj.* 直接的
introduce *v.* 介绍
disappointed *adj.* 失望

extra *adj.* 多余的
nervously *adv.* 紧张地

at all. For the past two years, her *counselor* had told her that the woodworking class she wanted to take was "just for boys."

"Mom, is there something you need to tell me?"

Mom sighed. "I don't know, honey. Things don't seem to be going like I imagined." She paused. Amanda knew that unlike Chris, Mom would always go on to explain what she meant, *even if* Amanda had already guessed. "I mean with Chris," Mom said.

"I like Chris. I like having him around," Amanda said.

"Well, I do, too, honey, but just being around isn't enough sometimes," Mom said. "You haven't talked about this with him, have you? No, you guys don't talk about anything," she said, answering her own question.

根本不介意这些。因为在过去的两年，她的辅导老师告诉她，她想要上的木工课是"只为男孩子们开设的"。

"妈妈，你有什么事要告诉我的吗？"

妈妈叹了口气，"我不知道，亲爱的，事情似乎并不像我想象的那样。"她停顿了一下。阿曼达知道妈妈和克里斯不同，她总是会继续解释她是什么意思的，即使阿曼达已经猜到了。"我的意思是和克里斯的事儿。"妈妈说。

"我喜欢克里斯。我喜欢有他在身边。"阿曼达说。

"哦，我也喜欢，亲爱的。但是有时只是在身边并不足够。"妈妈说，"你没和他谈论过这事儿，是吧？一定没有，你们两个从不谈论任何事情。"她自问自答地说着。

---

counselor *n.* 辅导老师

even if 即使

"No. We don't really need to talk," Amanda said.

The car stopped at a light and Mom took a deep breath in and out. "Well, I need someone to talk to. Another grown-up. And Chris just... well..." Mom trailed off. Amanda felt bad about having thought that her mother talked too much.

"Are you getting a divorce?" Amanda asked. Amanda was very *familiar* with divorce. Mom and Dad had gotten one when Amanda was barely three years old—so young that she didn't even *remember*. Then there was Mom's boyfriend, Chuck, with his blonde *mustache* and all his good *figures*. He was fun, and even though he and Mom were never married, it still hurt like a *divorce* when he left. Even Gram and Gramps were divorced, though they lived in the same building and still shouted at each other from their *porches* the way they had when they were married.

Mom started to *sniff* a bit, and she didn't answer. They pulled into a space in the MegaMart parking lot, and Mom reapplied her

---

"没谈过，我们并不真的需要交谈。"阿曼达说。

车子在红灯处停了下来，妈妈做了一个深呼吸，"好吧，我需要一个和我交谈的人。另一个成年人。而克里斯只是……好吧……"妈妈的声音越来越低。阿曼达感觉很糟糕，她认为她妈妈说得太多了。

"你们要离婚吗？"阿曼达问到。阿曼达对于离婚已经很熟悉了。在阿曼达刚满三岁的时候，爸爸妈妈就离婚了，因为年纪太小甚至都不记得了。后来是妈妈的男朋友，查克，有着金黄色的小胡子和很好的身材。他很有趣，尽管他并没有和妈妈结婚，可他的离去对阿曼达的伤害就好像是一次离婚。甚至爷爷和奶奶也离婚了，虽然他们还住在同一栋房子里，并且依然在他们当年结婚时候走过的门廊对着彼此大吼大叫。

妈妈开始有点抽噎，而她并没有回答我的问题。她们把车驶入美嘉玛

---

familiar *adj.* 熟悉的	remember *v.* 记得
mustache *n.* 胡子	figure *n.* 体形；身材
divorce *n.* 离婚	porch *n.* 门廊
sniff *v.* 抽鼻涕	

makeup in the *rearview mirror* before they got out and went inside the store. They shopped for hours before heading back home.

"We lost," was all Chris said when Amanda and Mom got home. Their shopping bags were filled with new, itchy clothes. As usual, Mom had tried to get Amanda to try on the pink shirts with all the *ribbons* and ruffles, but Amanda insisted on plain colors—red, blue, and green, and nothing *girly*. Amanda was going to ask what the score was, but if they'd lost, it really didn't matter much. Across the street, she saw her neighbor Cameron on a big pile of dirt, planting a stick into the top like a *flagpole* on a mountain.

"Going out to play," she shouted as she ran to join Cameron. The dirt pile had been left there when the town dug holes for new telephone poles, and the work crews had never come back to take it away.

超市停车场的停车位，在她们下车进到商店之前，妈妈对着后视镜补了一下妆。在动身回家之前，她们逛了好几个小时。

"我们输了。"当阿曼达和妈妈回到家时，克里斯就只说了这几个字。她们的袋子里装满了新的、让人发痒的衣服。和往常一样，妈妈让阿曼达试穿各种粉色带有绸带和褶边的衬衫，但是阿曼达却坚持穿素色的——红色的、蓝色的和绿色的，就是没有女孩子气的衣服。阿曼达本打算问问比分是多少，但是既然已经输了，比分真的没有多大意义了。街对面，她看见她的邻居卡梅隆在一大堆土上，正把一根树枝栽到土堆顶，好像山上的一个旗杆。

"我出去玩了。"她一边喊着一边跑出去加入了卡梅隆。这个土堆是城镇在挖新的电话线杆时留下的，而工人们再也没回来把土堆清理走。

---

rearview mirror（汽车等的）后视镜　　ribbon *n.* 绸带
girly *adj.* 像少女的　　flagpole *n.* 旗杆

"Where were you?" Cameron asked.

"School shopping," Amanda said.

"Did you get any cool stuff?" Cameron asked. "My mom said I could save my paper route money and get a graphing *calculator*."

"No, just clothes."

"Hmm." Cameron started *absentmindedly* smacking the dirt pile with his stick. Amanda had plans for the dirt pile. She'd wanted to make a fort by hollowing out the inside and building a long, low window facing the street. Then she was going to plant jungle-like plants all over the top to *camouflage* it. But Cameron never put up much of an effort, and he tore down half of what they'd done each time she went to Dad's for a weekend.

"You will be going to Hogan Junior, right? Now that your mom and Chris are married, you'll definitely be staying here and not going to your dad's for the school year, right?"

"Who knows how long they're going to be married," Amanda

"你去哪了？"卡梅隆问。

"去返校购物了。"阿曼达回答。

"买了什么很酷的东西吗？"卡梅隆问道。"我妈妈说我可以省下送报纸的钱，去买一个图形计算器。"

"没有，只买衣服了。"

"哦。"卡梅隆用他的棍子开始心不在焉地拍打着土堆。阿曼达对这个土堆早有计划。她想把这个土堆里面挖空做一个堡垒，造一个长长的、低矮的、面向街道的窗户。然后她打算在土堆上面种满丛林般的植物，把它伪装起来。但是卡梅隆根本没提供多大帮助，而且每次阿曼达去爸爸家过周末时，卡梅隆还会毁坏一半他们已经弄完的部分。

"你会去霍根中学，对吗？既然你妈妈和克里斯结婚了，你就肯定要

---

calculator *n.* 计算器
camouflage *v.* 伪装

absentmindedly *adv.* 心不在焉地

said. She dug some loose dirt out of what had almost been the *entrance* to their fort.

"Are you *serious*?" Cameron asked.

"That's what Mom said. She said that it wasn't like she imagined, and when I asked if they were getting divorced, she didn't say anything."

Cameron began carving *channels* down the side of the pile. "Hey, don't be mad at me when I say this," he said. He wiped his mouth with the back of his hand. "I never really liked Chris all that much. Chuck was more fun. Remember when he got all those bottle rockets for the Fourth of July?"

"I guess he was sort of more fun," Amanda said. "But Chris and I are more alike. We understand each other."

住在这里，学年期间也不用去你爸爸家了，对吗？"

"谁知道他们的婚能结多久？"阿曼达说。她从几乎成为他们堡垒入口的地方挖出一些松土。

"你说的是真的吗？"卡梅隆问。

"那是我妈妈说的。她说并不像她想象的那样，当我问他们是否会离婚时，她什么也没说。"

卡梅隆开始沿着土堆的一侧切出水渠。"嘿，我说这话你可别生气。"他用手背擦了擦嘴说："我其实并不怎么喜欢克里斯。查克要更有趣些。还记得七月四日他带了那么多的窜天猴吗？"

"我想他是那种很有趣的人，"阿曼达说，"但是我和克里斯更相像，我们相互理解。"

---

entrance *n.* 入口   serious *adj.* 认真的
channel *n.* 水渠

"He seems kind of *grumpy* sometimes," said Cameron.

"Well, I do, too," said Amanda, suddenly feeling kind of grumpy at Cameron. She didn't really hang out with him at school—just during summers, when they were the only kids in the *neighborhood*.

"I'm going to get an ice pop," Amanda said, without even bothering to offer Cameron one.

"Finished your fort?" Chris said when she stepped inside the house. He had the big TV taken apart all over the living room floor. It had been like that for a week now, but Amanda found that she liked watching Chris fix the TV almost as much as she had liked watching TV.

Amanda *kneeled down* next to the *disassembled* screen. "No. It never gets anywhere."

Chris pointed at the big TV tube. "*Radioactive*," he said. "Can't put it in the trash."

"*Dangerous*?" She asked.

"他有时似乎脾气暴躁。"卡梅隆说。

"其实，我也是啊。"阿曼达说着，突然感觉对卡梅隆有些生气。她在学校时其实并不和卡梅隆一起玩儿，只有在暑假的时候才混在一起，因为他们是街坊邻里中唯一的小孩子。

"我要去吃个冰棒。"阿曼达说着，根本不想费心给卡梅隆也拿一个。

"完成你的堡垒了？"阿曼达进到屋里时克里斯问。他在客厅地板上把大电视拆得到处都是。这个样子到现在已经一周了，但是阿曼达发现她喜欢看克里斯拆装电视如同她喜欢看电视一样。

阿曼达跪坐在拆下来的屏幕旁。"没有。反正它压根儿永远也不会完成。"

克里斯指着电视显像管，"有辐射。"他说道："不能把它扔到垃圾箱里。"

"危险吗？"阿曼达问。

---

grumpy *adj.* 脾气暴躁的
kneel down 跪下
radioactive *adj.* 放射性的

neighborhood *n.* 街坊
disassemble *v.* 拆开
dangerous *adj.* 危险的

"Not unless it's broken. You need help?"

She knew he was talking about the fort.

"Sure."

"Let's go," Chris said. And out they went.

Cameron was creating some kind of *battlefield* in his yard. He looked up and watched them, but didn't act like he wanted to join.

Chris and Amanda worked on the fort all that day. By *nightfall*, Amanda could get her whole body, except for her feet, inside the hollow they had carved. By the end of the weekend, Chris could crawl inside. By Wednesday, they leveled off the top so the roof wouldn't cave in.

"An arch is the strongest shape," Chris said. On Thursday, the ceiling took on a curve. By Friday, there was a long, *narrow* spy

---

"除非它破碎了，就不会危险。你需要帮忙吗？"
她知道他所指的是堡垒。
"当然。"
"我们走吧。"克里斯说道，接着他们就一起出门去了。
卡梅隆正在他家院子里创建着某种战场。他抬起头看着他们，但好像并没有想加入他们的意思。
克里斯和阿曼达一整天都努力地建造着堡垒。当夜幕降临时，阿曼达已经能把她的整个身体，除了脚以外，全都放到他们挖出的洞里了。到了周末，克里斯都能爬到里面去了。到星期三时，他们把顶部弄平整好让堡垒的屋顶不至于塌陷。
"拱形是最坚固的形状。"克里斯说。星期四，顶棚呈现出一条曲

---

battlefield *n.* 战场   nightfall *n.* 傍晚
narrow *adj.* 狭窄的

window looking out over the neighborhood. Cameron came by and helped smooth out the insides and level the floor.

Saturday morning, Amanda asked Mom if they could go to the plant store and buy some ferns and potted *tropical* trees to plant all over the fort.

"Absolutely not," she said.

"But, Mom—"

"First of all," Mom began, and Amanda rested her weight back on her heels in *preparation* for the lecture, "that dirt belongs to the city crew, not to us. Second, it's not even in our yard. Third, plants are *expensive* and we can't afford to buy them as toys. Fourth, they're just going to come along with *bulldozers* and smash the thing anyway."

线。到了星期五，堡垒有了一个狭长的窗户，通过它可以向外窥探整个住宅区。卡梅隆也过来帮忙把堡垒里面和地面都弄平整。

星期六的早上，阿曼达问妈妈说是否可以去植物商店，去买些蕨类植物和盆栽热带树，好种满整个堡垒。

"绝对不行。"她说。

"但是，妈妈……"

"首先，"妈妈开始她的训话了，而阿曼达则把重心向后移依托在脚后跟上，为她的演讲做好准备。"那土是属于市政工程队的，并不是属于我们的。第二，它甚至都不在我们的院子里。第三，植物很贵而我们无法负担像玩具一样买那些植物。第四，不管怎样它们将只会伴随着推土机的到来，并碾碎这东西。"

---

tropical *adj.* 热带的   preparation *n.* 准备
expensive *adj.* 贵的   bulldozer *n.* 推土机

"But the pile's been there for almost a year! It's almost done—it's the coolest thing." Amanda said.

"Don't *interrupt* me. You've spent every day out there in the mud, ruining the clothes we bought for school."

Amanda stuck out her bottom lip. "Chris may not talk a lot, but he sure knows me better than you do."

As soon as Amanda said it, she waited for Mom to be *furious* and start yelling at her. But instead, Mom's mouth just opened a little and she stared at Amanda with huge eyes. She didn't even cry.

"Go to your room," Mom said. Her voice sounded flat.

Amanda almost never cried, and she tried not to now, but there was already mud on her pillow—her tears had picked up dirt from her cheeks. She heard Mom moving pots around, getting ready to start dinner. She knew that Mom's mouth would be moving *silently*

"但这土堆在那儿已经将近一年了！堡垒就要建成了——它是最酷的东西。"阿曼达说道。

"别打断我。你已经把每一天都花费在外面的泥巴里了，把我们为开学准备的衣服都毁了。"

阿曼达撅起了她的下嘴唇。"克里斯也许并不怎么讲话，但他肯定比你要更加了解我。"

阿曼达一说完这句话，她就等着妈妈大发雷霆然后开始朝着她大吼大叫。但相反，妈妈的嘴巴只是张开了一点点，瞪着一双大眼睛目不转睛地盯着阿曼达。她甚至都没有哭。

"回你的房间去。"妈妈说。她的声音听起来很平淡。

阿曼达几乎从来没有哭过，而她现在也试着尽量不哭，但她的眼泪

---

interrupt *v.* 打断　　　　　　　　　　　　furious *adj.* 暴怒的
silently *adv.* 安静地

as she worked, like it always did when she was upset. Talking, talking, always talking. Every time Amanda thought about what she had said to Mom, she couldn't figure out *whether* she was sorry, or whether she had just been telling the truth.

She heard Chris go around the side of the house, turn on the hose, and rinse the dirt off his hands. That was another way that Amanda and Chris were different from Mom, but like each other. Amanda and Chris were always getting dirty doing things like working on the car, fixing the water *heater*, or putting in a new back step. Mom was always *complaining* about dirty hands. After the hose stopped, Chris's footsteps went around the house and inside.

"Where'did she go?" he asked.

"Who?" Mom said. There was another thing— Amanda and Chris always had to explain to Mom what they meant, but they always

---

流下来时混着脸颊上的尘土，已经在她的枕头上形成了泥巴。她听到妈妈在到处移动着坛坛罐罐，准备开始做晚饭。她知道当妈妈工作的时候会默默地念叨，就像她一直以来的那样，心烦的时候也会暗自默念。讲啊，讲啊，不停地讲话。每次阿曼达思索着她对妈妈说的话，都没办法断定她是否应该感到抱歉，抑或她只是在说出实情。

　　她听到克里斯绕到房子的侧面，打开水管，把泥土从他手上冲洗干净。那正是阿曼达和克里斯不同于妈妈之处，但却彼此相似的地方。阿曼达和克里斯在做事的时候常常会弄得脏兮兮的，例如修理汽车，安装热水器，或者是安置一个新的后踏板。妈妈总是在抱怨我们的脏手。关掉水管以后，克里斯的脚步声绕到了房子前面来到屋里。

　　"她去哪儿了？"他问道。

---

whether *conj.* 是否
complain *v.* 抱怨

heater *n.* 加热器

understood each other. Mom was always explaining things to them even after they got it.

"Amanda," Chris said.

Mom's voice got quiet, and Amanda couldn't hear what she said. They spoke back and forth for a moment, and then Chris's *footsteps* went down the hall to their bedroom. Amanda didn't hear anything but kitchen sounds for a while, so she figured that no one was going to come and talk to her after all. But then she heard the *doorknob* turn, and Chris came in.

Chris didn't say "Hello," or start asking her if she wanted to talk, like Mom always did. Amanda even found herself wondering why she couldn't just stay with Chris if he and Mom did get a divorce. He sat down in the chair by her bed. She didn't roll over to face him, and he didn't speak for a long time.

"You hurt your mom when you said that," he said. Amanda felt her tears start running down her cheeks again. She *wiped* them away,

---

"谁？"妈妈说。还有另外一件事——阿曼达和克里斯总是不得不向妈妈解释他们的意思，但他们通常能够明白彼此的意图。甚至在他们已经明白了之后，妈妈总是还要给他们作解释。

"阿曼达。"克里斯说。

妈妈的声音低了下来，阿曼达听不到她说些什么。他们你一言我一语地说了一阵子，然后克里斯的脚步声沿着走廊传向他们的卧室。一段时间里，阿曼达除了厨房传来的声音什么都听不到，所以她以为终归不会有人来和她谈话了。然而她却听到了门把手转动的声音，接着克里斯走了进来。

克里斯没有像妈妈通常做的那样，说"你好"，或者开始问她是否想要谈一谈。阿曼达甚至觉得自己很奇怪，如果他和妈妈真的离婚了，她为什么不能和克里斯待在一起呢。他在她床边的椅子上坐下。她并没有翻过身来面向他，而他也很长时间没有开口说话。

---

footstep *n.* 脚步声

doorknob *n.* 门把手

not wanting to get more dirt on her covers.

"She doesn't understand me," she said, whispering so that Chris wouldn't know she was crying.

"She knows what's best for you, and she loves you," Chris said.

"Then why can't she…"

"Sometimes people have a hard time talking to each other," Chris said. Amanda had to think about that for a minute. She knew it was true—she and Mom often did have a hard time talking to each other. She thought it was *awfully* strange that Mom, who talked so much, would find it difficult to talk to anyone.

Suddenly Amanda began to understand something about Mom: maybe talking was her way of trying to figure things out. Whenever Mom was giving her a talk or asking her too many questions, she really just wanted to understand. Amanda had never thought that

---

"你那样说的时候，伤害了你的妈妈。"他说。阿曼达感觉她的眼泪又开始从脸颊流了下来。她擦掉眼泪，不想在她的枕套上留下更多的污垢了。

"她不理解我。"她轻声说道，以便不让克里斯知道她在哭。

"她知道什么对你是最好的，而且她爱你。"克里斯说。

"那么她为什么不能……"

"有时人们很难相互沟通。"克里斯说。阿曼达不得不思考了一分钟。她知道这是真的——她和妈妈确实总是很难相互沟通。她认为这十分奇怪，就是妈妈，一个讲话如此之多的人，也会觉得与人交谈起来很困难。

突然阿曼达开始明白了关于妈妈的某些事情：也许交谈是她试图把事情弄清楚的方式。不论什么时候妈妈和她谈话或是问她过多的问题，她真的只是想要搞明白。阿曼达从来没有想过她尤其是难理解的，话说回来她

---

wipe *v.* 擦 awfully *adv.* 非常

she was *particularly* hard to understand, but then again maybe she was. She never really told Mom much of anything.

"I guess you understand Mom pretty well, don't you?" she asked Chris.

"I haven't been too great about it lately," he said. "She needs to get some *feedback* once in a while. And you need to *apologize*. Families have to work at staying together."

Amanda didn't nod or say anything. She knew Chris would *realize* that he had made his point. After a short time, he got up and left the room, closing the door behind him. Amanda sat up, blew her nose, and got ready to clean herself up to talk to Mom.

"Three *pickup* trucks, five cars, a telephone van, two dogs, and

就是很难理解的人。她从来没有真正地告诉妈妈任何事情的详细情况。

"我猜你一定非常了解妈妈，是吗？"她问克里斯。

"关于这事儿我一向都不是很在行。"他说。"她偶尔也需要得到一些反馈。而你需要道歉。家人必须为了能和睦生活在一起而努力。"

阿曼达没有点头或是说什么。她知道克里斯会意识到他已经讲出了问题的要害。过了一会儿，他站起来离开了房间，关上了身后的门。阿曼达坐了起来，擤了擤鼻涕，然后准备把自己梳洗干净去和妈妈谈话。

"三辆皮卡车，五辆轿车，一辆电话货车，两只狗，和一只鳄龟。"卡梅隆照着一张纸念着说："那些都是今天经过堡垒窗户的东西，而它们中没有一个知道我在这里。这个地方真是太棒了！你去哪儿了？"阿曼达刚刚到达那个土堆，他就问道。

---

particularly *adv.* 特别地   feedback *n.* 反馈

apologize *v.* 道歉   realize *v.* 认识到

pickup *n.* 皮卡车

a snapping *turtle*," Cameron said, reading from a sheet of paper. "Those are all the things that passed by the fort window today, and not one of them knew I was in here. This place is great! Where have you been?" he asked. Amanda had just arrived at the dirt pile.

"Mom and I went to get our nails done," Amanda said.

"Really? So we can't plant the *vines* after all, since you won't want to mess your nails up." Cameron sounded disappointed.

"No. I made a deal with my mom. I would go and have a 'salon day' with her if she came outside and helped us plant camouflage this afternoon."

"No way!"

"Watch out!" came a voice from outside the dirt fort. Suddenly, a *splash* of water came in through the window. Mom was dragging the hose across the road. "Can't plant things if the soil's not wet!" She aimed the *sprayer* right in the fort, and Cameron and Amanda ran outside, muddy and wet, *screaming* with laughter.

"妈妈和我去做指甲了。"阿曼达说。

"真的吗？所以我们终究是不能种藤蔓了，因为你不会想把你的指甲弄坏的。"卡梅隆听起来很失望。

"不，我和妈妈达成了一个协议。如果她今天下午到外面来，并帮我们种上伪装的话，我就和她一起过一个'美容院日'。"

"不能吧！"

"留神！"从泥土碉堡外面传来了一个声音。突然，飞溅的水花从窗户喷了进来。妈妈正拖着水管穿过马路。"如果土壤不潮湿，就不能种东西！"她把喷头正对着堡垒里面，卡梅隆和阿曼达都跑到了外面，浑身湿透，满身泥巴，笑得前仰后合。

---

turtle *n.* 龟

splash *n.* 飞溅的水

scream *v.* 尖叫

vine *n.* 藤蔓

sprayer *n.* 喷雾器